DATE DUE	RETURNED

Monsieur d'Eon

Monsieur d'Eon

by
Mark Brownell

Playwrights Canada Press
Toronto•Canada

Monsieur d'Eon © Copyright 1998 Mark Brownell

Playwrights Canada Press
54 Wolseley Street, 2nd Floor
Toronto, Ontario CANADA M5T 1A5
416-703-0201   fax 416-703-0059
info@puc.ca   http://www.puc.ca

Playwrights Canada Press acknowledges the support of
The Canada Council for the Arts for our publishing programme and
the Ontario Arts Council.

ONTARIO ARTS COUNCIL
CONSEIL DES ARTS DE L'ONTARIO

Production Editor: Jodi Armstrong

National Library of Canada Cataloguing in Publication Data

Brownell, Mark
    Monsieur d'Eon

A play.
ISBN 0-88754-607-2

I. Title

PS8553.R6915M66   2001   C812'.6   C00-932030-X
PR9199.4.B76M66   2001

First edition: May 2001
Printed and bound by AGMV-Marquis at Quebec, Canada.

To Professor Gary Kates, with thanks and appreciation.

Monsieur d'Eon was first produced at Buddies in Bad Times Theatre, Toronto in 1998. This production received four Dora Mavor Moore nominations. It featured the following cast:

Christine Brubaker
Mark Christmann
Robert Clarke
Stuart Clow
David Fraser
Martin Julien
Ron Kennell
Kate Lynch
Jane Moffat
Christopher Sawchyn

Directed by Sue Miner
Costume and Set Design by Lori Hickling
Lighting Design by Philip Cygan
Original Music Composition by Steve Thomas
Choreography by Robert McCollum
Fight Choreography by Michael Chipman
Stage Managed by Hilary Unger

CHARACTERS (in order of appearance):

Jeanne d'Arc – an apparition
A Young d'Eon – 7-8 years old
A Court Servant – announcer
King Louis XV of France
Prince de Conti (Louis-François de Bourbon)
Mme. Pompadour – Louis XV's Lover and Pimp
Charles François, Comte de Broglie – d'Eon's patron

Chevalier(e) d'Eon de Beaumont (Charles-Geneviève-Louise-August-André-Thimothée d'Eon) – our hero

The Macaroni Brothers – two court fops
The King's Secret Chorus – three shadowy men
Elizabeth I – Empress of Russia
Catherine the Great – a young girl
Prince de Soubise – a Bourbon – rival of Conti
King George III of England
Comte de Guerchy – French Ambassador to England
Pierre-Henri Treyssac de Vergy – Guerchy's assistant
John Wilkes – d'Eon's English friend and Second
Sopwith – Halifax's capable servant
Lord Halifax – English foreign minister
Lord Mansfield – a judge
Lawyer – for the prosecution
Louis XVI – grandson of Louis XV
Pierre-Augustin Caron de Beaumarchais – the famous playwright
Jean-Jacques Rousseau – the famous philosopher
Charles Théveneau de Morande – publisher of scandal sheets and liaison to Beaumarchais
Bookies – three odds-givers at Lloyds of London
Rose Bertin – a fashionable dress-designer
Her Assistant
Marie-Antoinette – wife of Louis XVI
Casanova – himself
The Marquis de Sade – himself
Benjamin Franklin – himself
Anacharsis Cloots – a citizen of the French Revolution
The Mad Jailer of the Bastille – a blood-thirsty half-wit
The Prince of Wales – son of George III
Drunk – a duelist
Mrs. Cole – an old woman – d'Eon's roommate
A Friend – a younger woman
A Priest

PROLOGUE

1736. A scorching summer day in the region of Tonnerre. A child D'EON enters carrying some buckets of water. He stops and stares at a shimmering JEANNE d'Arc. She blocks his path.

D'EON   Hello, shiny lady.

JEANNE   Hello, d'Eon. You're in such a rush today.

D'EON   I'm helping out in the fields. The grapevines need water or they turn to dust and blow away.

JEANNE   If you pray to me, I will make sure that heaven rains upon your vines.

D'EON   That is very kind of you. I will pray to you. Thank you. *(bows)*

JEANNE   You're welcome.

D'EON   ...what name should I pray to?

JEANNE smiles.

Are you my guardian angel?

JEANNE   No. I am you. Do you understand?

D'EON   My father says I'm too young to understand anything.

JEANNE   You will understand who I am one day.

D'EON   I already know who you are. You're the maiden that I read about in my picture books.

JEANNE   That's right. And do you know what a maiden is?

D'EON   Someone who hasn't had babies.

JEANNE	That's right. Someone who has taken a vow.
D'EON	Never to have babies.
JEANNE	To be a virgin.
D'EON	Our Lord's mother was a blessed virgin.
JEANNE	She certainly was.
D'EON	Should I be a virgin too?
JEANNE	You should if you want to be like me.
D'EON	You're very beautiful.
JEANNE	Thank you. You are beautiful too.

They touch each other's faces.

D'EON	Thank you. Will I always be so beautiful? Let me see!
JEANNE	There's a price to pay for that – to see what's in your future.
D'EON	I'll pay it. I have two livres saved up.
JEANNE	Come then. Take my hand – and see what you will be.

Young D'EON touches her hand – a blinding light and fanfare. Scene change as the court of LOUIS the XVth of France streams in through an upstage opening.

SERVANT	All bow for the coming of His Royal Majesty King Louis the Fifteenth, Supreme Ruler of all France, Grande Overseer of the Colonies of North America, Rightful and Legitimate Heir of Louis Fourteen Sun King, Commander General of all French Forces, World Conqueror, Royal Countenance Unsurpassed, Radiant Visage, He Alone Blessed by God

and Pope to forward France to the ultimate glory of the coming of...

LOUIS XV is revealed – a petulant man with a large hangover. He claps his hands.

LOUIS   Shut up! That's enough cow shit for today. (*He slumps on his throne.*) Orders of the day. Hurry up. My time is precious. You people should be paying me more for this thankless job. Well, what are you all staring at? You think it's easy being King? Conti, do you think so?

CONTI   I imagine that it is very difficult for your Majesty.

LOUIS   But, of course, not for you, Cousin. You'd love to take my place, wouldn't you?

CONTI   Never, Sire.

LOUIS   Liar! Fortunately I'm working on another throne for you – close enough to Versailles but far enough away that I don't have to look at that handsome face of yours every day.

CONTI   My cousin toys with me.

LOUIS   If only you knew the sacrifices I make for you.

POMPADOUR   They don't pay you enough, Louis.

LOUIS   That's right. You're not farting in the wind about that, my dear. Worries. Worries like stones on my head.

POMPADOUR   I'll anoint that head in oils tonight.

LOUIS   I hope that's not all you'll be anointing, my dear. (*smacks his lips*)

POMPADOUR	No indeed. I have some exotic Egyptian oils concocted especially for the royal scepter.
LOUIS	Oooo. Clear the court! I have some private business with the Royal Sweetie-pie.
SERVANT	Clear the court!

Courtiers begin to file out.

POMPADOUR	Not now, dear *Frérot*. You've got business to attend to.
SERVANT	Come back! Not yet!

Courtiers hurriedly re-enter.

LOUIS	Oh bugger. No rest for the wicked. You are my better half, *ma Pompadourette*. What would I do without you? (*makes slurping kissy noises*)
POMPADOUR	Rot in Hell, your Royal Majesty.

They start to make love, much to the embarrassment of the court.

LOUIS	Alright. No need to gawk, you perverts. Introductions. Chop, chop.
SERVANT	The Brothers Macaroni.

MACARONI Brothers come forward and bow elaborately. LOUIS cuts them off before they can speak.

LOUIS	Next!
SERVANT	Charles François, Comte de Broglie.

BROGLIE approaches and kneels.

LOUIS	I'm surprised you can even kneel this morning.

BROGLIE	Had I been drinking from any wine-cellar other than the King's last night, I would have my head in a chamber pot this very moment.
LOUIS	State your business.
BROGLIE	As I mentioned last night, Majesty...
LOUIS	How can I remember what occurred last night? The very same wine-cellar that saves you from vomiting robs me of my wits.
BROGLIE	Never forgetful, sire. I merely mentioned offhand that I would like to make an introduction. It wasn't worthy of your memory.
LOUIS	Proceed.
BROGLIE	Come forward, d'Eon. Greet His Majesty, the King.

The crowd mumbles. D'EON approaches and bows with an elaborate flourish then kneels.

MACARONI 1	Who *is* he?
MACARONI 2	Such a fetching leg.
MACARONI 1	Such a soft countenance.
MACARONI 2	Hardly a hair out of place...
MACARONI 1	And so soft of cheek, skin like ivory...
MACARONI 2	Obviously from old blood.
MACARONI 1	Nobility. I most heartily agree...
MACARONI 2	But a touch of the provincial.
MACARONI 1	He hides it well though.
MACARONI 2	Yes.

LOUIS	Shut up, you Macaronis! Please proceed, Comte.
BROGLIE	Majesty, may I introduce to you... Monsieur Charles-Geneviève-Louise-August-André-Thimothée d'Eon.
D'EON	Your Royal Majesty.

D'EON debases himself still further.

LOUIS	You may simply kneel in my presence, d'Eon. It's not necessary to kiss the royal tiles.
D'EON	I offer myself completely to his Royal Majesty.
LOUIS	Yes, yes. Where are you from?
D'EON	Tonnerre, Majesty.
LOUIS	Never heard of it.
BROGLIE	A small town in Burgundy, Sire. Noted for its excellent vineyards.
LOUIS	It comes back to me now. Although I've drunk so much Burgundy that it's a miracle I can remember anything at all.
D'EON	A good Tonnerre doesn't damage the memory, Majesty. It livens the spirit. It lengthens life.
LOUIS	Oh really. Well, in my humble opinion wine doesn't lengthen anything. Right, Pompadour?
POMPADOUR	Never, your lengthiness. Your tumescence is legendary.
D'EON	If I may be so bold, Sire, I offer you half of this year's harvest as payment for this introduction.

BROGLIE Don't be gauche, d'Eon.

LOUIS Oh, don't stop him piling on the bribes. Excellent. Very well! I shall drain your vineyards dry. What else do you have to give for the honour of being in my august presence?

D'EON ...nothing... but myself, sire. And my sword.

He draws it and lays it at LOUIS' feet.

LOUIS (*scoffs*) Another fanatic. Away with him. I've got fanatics aplenty who are ready to eat grapeshot should I order it.

BROGLIE Don't be fooled by d'Eon's fervour, Majesty. He has a bright young head on his shoulders.

LOUIS You're his patron. You have to say stuff like that. (*rises*) Everyone here has forgotten that we are going to war soon. I need men with brains. Arise, d'Eon. Good luck with whatever it is you will be doing in...

BROGLIE I thought his Majesty might set young d'Eon a special task.

LOUIS Special?

BROGLIE (*touches his nose*) Special.

LOUIS Clear the court! I have some private business to attend to.

SERVANT Clear the court!

The courtiers file out but POMPADOUR remains. BROGLIE clears his throat.

LOUIS What? Oh, yes. Pompadour. You must go as well. This won't take long, dearest. You'd be bored. It's... men stuff.

POMPADOUR	...very well. I'll be in my chambers.
LOUIS	You go warm up those Egyptian oils!
POMPADOUR	Don't be too long.

She exits.

LOUIS	She'll bury me, that Gypsy minx.
BROGLIE	Very ambitious.
LOUIS	In this nest of rats – who isn't?
BROGLIE	It might not be judicious to trust a woman who has...

BROGLIE stops, realizing that he has gone too far.

LOUIS	Who has what?! I'll not hear another word said against her – unless you'd enjoy a nice long exile in the swamps of Louisiana.
BROGLIE	Certainly not, sire.
LOUIS	She blows my horn – that's all that matters to me.
BROGLIE	Evidently, sire.
LOUIS	Let's move on to business. What makes you think I have use for this little grape seed?
BROGLIE	d'Eon is from good stock. A family of ancient heritage. His mother has educated him well in the ways of the sword and the salon.
LOUIS	So you say.
D'EON	I live only to serve his Majesty.
LOUIS	He seems fawning enough for what I have in mind.

BROGLIE   Indeed.

LOUIS   ...and... what was it that I had in mind for him?

BROGLIE   To travel to the Court of Russia, Sire. To instruct the Empress Elizabeth in the ways of a civilized French court.

LOUIS   That's right! What do you say to that, d'Eon? Are you up to teaching a bunch of Cossacks how to eat with a fork?

D'EON   Wherever your Majesty sends me – there I shall serve.

LOUIS   They're barbarians, you know. They'll smash your testicles if you give 'em a sideways glance.

D'EON   I am prepared to die for my King.

LOUIS   That's good – because you probably will.

BROGLIE   It is a sensitive position, d'Eon. The King intends to put his cousin on the Polish throne. To do this we will need Russia's assistance. We wish you to pour honey into Elizabeth's ear.

D'EON   As you command.

LOUIS   Yes, yes. Good, good. I have no more time for this. Pompadour will be getting impatient. Induct him. Now I'm off to get my knob polished. You may rise exactly two minutes after I am gone. (*He exits.*)

D'EON   My Lord?

   BROGLIE signals silence. The King's Secret Chorus enters – they are a shadowy group of caped/masked men who seem to be joined

> *together in one body. They signal D'EON and BROGLIE with sacred Masonic symbols.*

BROGLIE You are to be inducted into the King's Secret, d'Eon. It is quite an honour.

SECRET 1 The Clandestine Order of the King's Secret.

SECRET 2 A shadowy yet powerful web of intelligence gathering activity formed by His Royal Majesty.

SECRET 3 A cabal of operatives deeply entrenched in every country of the civilized world.

SECRET 1 You will only know us by our secret symbol...

ALL The Black Pomegranate!

> *They all produce black pomegranates.*

BROGLIE From the King's secret orchards, d'Eon. There is no other like it in the world.

SECRET 1 All members of The King's Secret carry The Black Pomegranate.

SECRET 2 The secret symbol of the Secret society.

SECRET 3 The secret key that unlocks all of our secrets.

SECRET 1 Trust no one who does not bear The Black Pomegranate.

D'EON What's to stop someone from painting an ordinary pomegranate black?

BROGLIE Shut up, d'Eon! The Black Pomegranate isn't something to make fun of!

> *Broglie signals the Secret Chorus to leave. They exit with many secret hand-signals.*

You will learn respect. It is the King's Secret Society that protects us all from Madame Pompadour.

D'EON   But...

BROGLIE   Too many questions come out of your head, d'Eon. If you want to keep it on your shoulders then you will do as you are told.

D'EON   I am yours to command.

BROGLIE   Good, my boy. You are under Secret orders. You will proceed immediately to...

Light change – more pageantry.

SERVANT   The Court of the Empress Elizabeth of Russia.

A Russian folk-dance. Cossack courtiers enter, all cross-dressed but unmasked. D'EON enters with ELIZABETH.

ELIZABETH   Well, Monsieur. What do you think of my little masquerade ball?

D'EON   Heavenly, Empress. You are unsurpassed in...

ELIZABETH   You want to say "gaudiness".

D'EON   Certainly not. Call it *panache* or call it nothing.

ELIZABETH   I like to take fashion risks.

D'EON   You would not be in the envy of Europe's clothiers if you did not. They trail in your dust.

CATHERINE appears with a cup of wine.

CATHERINE   Ah yes, have I introduced you to my ward, Catherine?

D'EON   I haven't yet had the pleasure.

CATHERINE	Would you care for some wine, Monsieur.
D'EON	Offered from the hands of a princess? How could I refuse?
CATHERINE	It isn't the caliber of a French wine, Monsieur, but it will serve its purpose.
D'EON	Ambrosia, I'm sure.

> *D'EON puts it to his lips but ELIZABETH stops him.*

ELIZABETH	A word of caution. Never accept any gift of food or drink from Catherine without seeing her taste it first.
CATHERINE	Auntie...
ELIZABETH	The child has developed a rather nasty interest in chemistry.
CATHERINE	(*takes the cup from D'EON*) I would never dream of poisoning him, Auntie.

> *She touches the cup to her lips but doesn't drink. She then gives it to a servant who takes it cautiously away.*

	You have embarrassed me in front of our guest.
ELIZABETH	Run along to your stables, darling. Your horses will be wanting attention.
CATHERINE	My horses are more civilized company than you are. (*She exits.*)
ELIZABETH	I apologize for her behaviour, d'Eon.
D'EON	She is charming.
ELIZABETH	She is *German*. I have tried to guide her to the civilized ways of Mother Russia. I have

treated her like a daughter but still she reverts to German barbarity. What a burden it is to raise children. Have you any of your own?

D'EON   I am unmarried, Empress.

ELIZABETH   So?

D'EON   And I am childless.

ELIZABETH   Are you a virgin then?

D'EON   (*blushing*) Yes, Empress.

ELIZABETH   A virgin from the French court!

D'EON   Indeed I am, Empress.

ELIZABETH   You are a precious commodity. I will send you twenty food-testers in the morning.

D'EON   I'm sure that won't be necessary.

ELIZABETH   Don't worry. They are peasants. They are always happy to fill their bellies.

D'EON   You are most generous.

ELIZABETH   Yes, I know. If you have any other needs, just ask.

D'EON   I have a question, Empress. Why are your courtiers not masked?

ELIZABETH   Why should they be?

D'EON   Well, at Versailles many of our court would feel embarrassed to openly dress as the opposite sex without the security of a mask to hide behind.

ELIZABETH   I order them to be unmasked! It is a show of my power over them. Observe...

> *She claps her hands – the dance stops and all the courtiers listen attentively.*

I present to you all Monsieur d'Eon! Clap gently in his honour.

> *They all clap.*

Monsieur d'Eon travelled many gruelling miles from the court of Versailles to be with us here this evening. Grovel on the ground like dogs to show him how happy you are that he has arrived safely.

> *All the courtiers immediately get down on all fours and grovel.*

You see? They are all peasants. They will do as they are told. More dancing!

> *She claps her hands – the dance begins again.*

Stop dancing! It is important for an Empress to maintain complete control of her court. Tell me. Is it true that you French have outlawed a woman sitting on the throne?

D'EON   True.

ELIZABETH   Detestable!

D'EON   A French woman would prefer to rule the salon – where true power is found.

ELIZABETH   Why should women hide behind their fans? We have a natural strength that can always transcend a man. Observe. Kneel before me.

D'EON   *(kneels)* Empress?

ELIZABETH   You are a man, d'Eon. You are in my court. Why should you be any different from these half-men of Mother Russia? I order you to dress as a woman.

D'EON	But, Empress... I cannot do this.
ELIZABETH	Why not? I order you to do it.
D'EON	I respectfully cannot...
ELIZABETH	What?!
D'EON	...because... I *am* a woman.
ELIZABETH	(*shocked, but then snickers*) You are a woman?
D'EON	Yes, Empress... and so should therefore dress like a man in your presence.
ELIZABETH	(*laughs*) Wonderful! Wonderful! You French men are so devious.
D'EON	Please forgive my jest, I...
ELIZABETH	(*slapping him roughly on the back*) No need to apologize, d'Eon. We "women" should stick together, yes? You shall instruct me in the ways of French femininity! Now come. Tell me about... Paris...

> *A flourish of music. Light change – cut to LOUIS and BROGLIE.*

LOUIS	Ho ho! Then he claimed he was a woman! Excellent! Slipped off her meat hook with that one!
BROGLIE	Yes, Majesty.
LOUIS	Elizabeth is such a Cossack. I fucked her, you know!
BROGLIE	Yes, sire. d'Eon then goes on to say that we have Elizabeth's complete support in our upcoming conflict with Prussia. He encloses a rough draft of a secret treaty.

LOUIS   Stupendous. He's been an excellent choice. A quick thinker. That's the sort of man I need to handle my affairs abroad. I'm glad I thought of him.

BROGLIE   Your Majesty made an excellent decision. What are your orders?

LOUIS   Call him back at once!

BROGLIE   I have already had the foresight, Majesty.

LOUIS   Then send him in!

BROGLIE   (*bows*) At once, Sire.

> *D'EON enters triumphant into the court of LOUIS.*

LOUIS   d'Eon, were I Caesar I would parade you about in a chariot.

D'EON   His majesty does me a great service by merely mentioning my name.

LOUIS   Such humility. That's what I like to hear. Humility saves me money. How would you like a position in the Dragoons?

D'EON   Sire! (*bowing lower*)

BROGLIE   It's war, d'Eon. Prussia and Britain have attacked our armies in the Rhine. You will join me as a Captain in the Dragoons.

LOUIS   This will be a quick engagement. Frederick has no stomach for an extended fight. We'll kick their fat German arses across the Rhine and smash the Brits in Poland. With Conti safely tucked away on the Polish throne, French influence will extend clear to St. Petersburg.

BROGLIE	This will be an excellent opportunity for you to reap some military glory, d'Eon.
LOUIS	With a tidy little military pension to follow.
D'EON	I don't care for pensions, Majesty, I wish only to fight for my King.
LOUIS	Yes, yes. Of course. Well Broglie, I order you to marshall our forces immediately and push the Hun back across the Rhine. I prophesy that you will destroy them in a month. I can feel it in my swelling bone.
BROGLIE	A month? Perhaps your Majesty is being overly optimistic.
LOUIS	Nonsense. Use this handkerchief to mop up the French blood. You will prevail over Frederick's pitiful armies. After all, what do Prussians know about fighting?

> *The sound of a cannonball rocketing overhead. Various explosions and lighting change as a group of French nobles gather on a hillside overlooking the battle of Villingshausen. D'EON looks at the battle through a spyglass. SOUBISE and BROGLIE bicker.*

D'EON	Our forces have been split in two.
SOUBISE	Naturally. That was my plan from the start.
BROGLIE	We will live to regret this decision, Soubise.
SOUBISE	Nonsense. I know exactly what I'm doing. We outnumber the Prussian forces two-to-one. It is a natural pincer movement.
BROGLIE	The Prussians fight unconventionally.
SOUBISE	I have studied the sauerkraut-eaters strategy. It is classic Spartan manœuvering.

BROGLIE	Any comparison is purely academic. They have managed to survive six years of our assaults and their kingdoms still remain intact.

A stray bullet knocks off the wig of a nobleman. He screams and runs off.

D'EON	The battle is shifting this way.
SOUBISE	We'd best make for higher ground.

Another stray bullet. Another nobleman flees.

D'EON	They have captured our guns on the opposite hill.
SOUBISE	(*edging away*) Um... we'll all be safer up the hill.
D'EON	(*to BROGLIE*) Why did the King appoint this moron?
BROGLIE	It was Pompadour's decision.

Another bullet. A nobleman dies with a musket-ball through his eye.

SOUBISE	Shall we be going?
BROGLIE	Don't you wish to sound the retreat?
SOUBISE	They'll all be dead soon. Why bother?
BROGLIE	It is your duty.
SOUBISE	I am a Prince of the Blood. I will never sound the retreat.
BROGLIE	Then relinquish your command.
SOUBISE	Gladly. You are now in command, Broglie. You shall bear the blame for this defeat. (*He exits.*)

BROGLIE	d'Eon.
D'EON	Commander?
BROGLIE	Sound the retreat.
D'EON	At once, Commander (*He signals.*)
BROGLIE	It seems that we are the only nobles remaining.
D'EON	There are many brave soldiers still fighting on the battlefield.
BROGLIE	Let's make for safety.
D'EON	You will need a rear guard, Charles. I will remain.
BROGLIE	There is no need to fight. You are not obligated.
D'EON	I joined the Dragoons to fight. So far I have done nothing but pour wine and wet-nurse the Prince de Soubise. Allow me to fight now.
BROGLIE	You'll get your arse shot off.
D'EON	Rather my arse than yours, Charles. (*draws his sword and salutes*)
BROGLIE	My arse thanks you, d'Eon. *Bonne chance.*
	They embrace. The noise of the battle increases.
D'EON	...I love you, Charles.
BROGLIE	d'Eon. (*kissing him twice on the cheek*) There is no greater love than a soldier's love to his fellow soldier in battle.
D'EON	No, I mean... I truly love you.

BROGLIE	I know. Manly love is everything. *Vive la France!* (*He runs away from the battle.*)

The noise increases. D'EON rushes forward with sword held high. A sudden silence. JEANNE d'Arc appears in battle gear.

JEANNE	Are you ready, d'Eon? It's a fine day for killing.
D'EON	Yes, shiny lady.
JEANNE	Are you afraid of dying?
D'EON	Not as long as you are with me.
JEANNE	I am always with you, d'Eon. Are you ready to kill some Prussians?
D'EON	Ready.
JEANNE	Come, lift your sword and feel my strength added to yours.
D'EON	(*He lifts his sword and feels a rush of confidence.*) I love you.
JEANNE	Then you love yourself.

A lighting change suggesting dark storm clouds. D'EON slices into the enemy line with slow passes of his sword.

D'EON	For the King I fight today. Le Roi. To the glory of France. And my destiny. May she guide my sword to the heart of my enemy. May God reveal my terrible presence this day. May they know who I truly am in spirit and in body as I cut them down like straw men. They look in my eyes and see their own deaths. They also see who slays them. *La Pucelle!*

A furious commotion of battle. He is swept away. A lighting change. The Court of Louis

XV. BROGLIE stands accused of botching the Prussian campaign. D'EON stands behind him with a bandaged arm.

POMPADOUR Seven hundred and fifty-seven dead. More than one thousand wounded. One thousand one-hundred and forty three taken prisoner. All told three-thousand soldiers lost – double the number of Prussians.

LOUIS Who is to blame for this?

POMPADOUR Well, you certainly can't blame Soubise, Louis. He wasn't even in command at the time the retreat was sounded.

BROGLIE I was in command.

LOUIS Then you are to blame.

BROGLIE If his Majesty says so.

LOUIS Well I do say so, you impertinent puppy. You are to blame. You are to be punished.

POMPADOUR He should be executed.

LOUIS Chopped? Oh no, no. That's far too harsh. Step forward, Broglie. You are to be court marshalled immediately. I strip you of all military titles and stipends.

POMPADOUR Banish him.

LOUIS Banish? Yes. I banish you... to your estate in Normandy.

POMPADOUR You are far too lenient. Exile him.

LOUIS I'll be the judge of whether I'm too lenient, my dear. Off to Normandy, Broglie. Quick like a bunny – out of my sight.

> *BROGLIE bows and leaves. D'EON follows him.*

LOUIS And where do you think you are going, d'Eon?

D'EON I naturally thought that...

LOUIS You haven't been dismissed by your sovereign. Kneel before me.

> *D'EON kneels.*

Word of your courageous actions at Villingshausen has reached our ear.

D'EON Sire?

LOUIS Your patron is banished, but you are not. I am told that it would have been a total rout if you had not rallied the troops at the last moment.

D'EON I merely sounded the retreat, Majesty.

LOUIS You were wounded in battle twice and yet fought on. For that bravery I award you a titlement. Arise now, Chevalier d'Eon de Beaumont.

D'EON I am speechless, Sire. I certainly don't deserve...

LOUIS I'll be the judge of what you do and don't deserve. No doubt you also don't deserve a posting to the British court. I've had it up to here with this war, d'Eon. It's been seven years and it's cost me one billion livres. You shall join our diplomatic team and negotiate the peace. You did such a wonderful job with the Empress; I need your honeyed tongue once again.

D'EON What can I say...

LOUIS	Don't say anything. Keep you mouth shut until you get to England, then open it wide. Be off now with my royal blessing.
	All exit except D'EON and POMPADOUR. Unaware of her presence, he kneels in silent prayer.
POMPADOUR	Congratulations, d'Eon.
D'EON	Madame.
POMPADOUR	You have been avoiding me.
D'EON	With good cause. I was told that you were not to be trusted.
POMPADOUR	Poison words from your patron.
D'EON	You tried to kill us.
POMPADOUR	I thought Soubise was the right choice. I made a mistake.
D'EON	Forgive me, but you do not have a reputation for making mistakes.
POMPADOUR	I thank you for that, but I am fallible just like any other woman.
D'EON	You are not just any woman, Madame.
POMPADOUR	We don't need to be enemies. Now that Broglie is banished you will need a friend like me.
D'EON	In truth, the only friend I need is God.
POMPADOUR	God is not to be found in the court of Louis.
D'EON	God is everywhere, Madame. Even in this whorehouse. I pray that someday God will reveal his love to you.

POMPADOUR   And who do you love, d'Eon? Besides God, that is.

D'EON   I try to love everyone, Madame. Just as Jesus instructed us to do.

POMPADOUR   That's not the sort of love I'm talking about.

D'EON   If Madame's network of spies is as formidable as they say, then you already know the answer to that question.

POMPADOUR   My spies tell me that you are a virgin.

D'EON   That is between God and myself, Madame.

POMPADOUR   I won't insult you then, by offering my services in bed in exchange for your devotion.

D'EON   You are far too sophisticated a woman for such a gauche manœuver.

POMPADOUR   Accept a small token from an enemy then, a portrait...

She gives him a small portrait of herself.

Keep it close to you... to remember that I gave you a choice.

A lighting change. She exits leaving D'EON alone once again. He kneels in silent prayer. Members of the King's Secret enter with a masked BROGLIE.

SECRET 1   Very pious, d'Eon.

SECRET 3   It will take more than prayer to your false Papist god to save you from Madame Pompadour.

D'EON   What would a bunch of Freemasons know about the power of prayer? You're all atheists.

SECRET 1	We are free-thinkers.
D'EON	Free-thinkers who can't even travel by light of day.
SECRET 3	We must remain clandestine.
D'EON	Yes, I never would have guessed it was you behind that silly mask, Saint-Germain. And you, Tercier. How is that rash of yours? Still keeping you from... (*He makes a lewd gesture.*)
SECRET 1	Hold your tongue, d'Eon!
D'EON	Why should I? You are all nothing with my patron banished. You must scurry about in the shadows like masked rats.
BROGLIE	(*taking off his mask*) Am I a rat too?
D'EON	Charles!? I thought...
BROGLIE	The King's Secret is alive and well; we have orders for you.
D'EON	I already have orders from the King.
BROGLIE	These are counter orders... (*hands him a scroll with the King's seal*) ...signed by the King, himself. You will negotiate the peace but you will also scout the British coast for a suitable spot.
D'EON	What sort of spot?
SECRETS	Invasion!
BROGLIE	The King intends to invade Britain.
D'EON	Is he planning on taking anyone with him?
BROGLIE	That tongue of yours will be your undoing.

SECRET 1 breaks the seal. LOUIS speaks from another part of the stage...

LOUIS
"...d'Eon will receive my orders through the Comte de Broglie concerning the reconnaissance for the invasion of England. My intention is that he keep this affair strictly secret and that he never mention anything of it to any living person, not even to my ministers."

BROGLIE
That letter is your security. While you are in possession of it you are protected from your enemies.

D'EON
I'm growing very tired of this game, Charles. Why must the King have contrary policies?

BROGLIE
He thinks it's clever.

D'EON
He puts us all in great danger. Who must I obey should orders conflict?

BROGLIE
Me, of course. I am your conduit to the King. Follow me and I will ensure that you become acting ambassador to the British Court.

SECRET 1
It is a marvelous opportunity, d'Eon.

SECRET 2
Your influence will be unsurpassed.

BROGLIE
You will embark now. We of the Secret give you our very special blessing. (*They proffer the pomegranate.*) Go with all speed to...

GEORGE
The Court of King George III!

A lighting change. The Court of George III. D'EON and a handful of French emissaries bow to an empty throne. GEORGE enters and looks distracted.

Oh bugger, that's me! (*He adjusts his wig.*) Wilkomen! Wilkomen, my French friends!

Mumbled responses from the French.

Now what's all this about, d'Eon?
Negotiations bogging down, no doubt.

D'EON   A few minor snags, Majesty. You still hold
18,000 of our countrymen prisoner in New
France.

GEORGE   "New France"? Last time I checked the map
I didn't see any country called "New France".

English courtiers laugh.

D'EON   Your Majesty makes a joke.

GEORGE   Ha ha! Shouldn't needle you like that. I
apologize. Well then. 18,000 – that's quite
a lot of Frenchmen sitting on their duffs,
scarfing up my good British cooking.

D'EON   Punishment enough.

French laugh.

GEORGE   What was that?

D'EON   ...we hope to... push enough for their release
so that they are no longer a burden to your
Majesty.

GEORGE   What do you offer in exchange for their
release?

D'EON   His Majesty must realize that the French
coffers are not full enough to pay ransom for
such a large number.

GEORGE   Just so. Well... hmm.... Ah! The perfect
solution. Destroy your harbour at Dunkirk.
That will suffice.

D'EON   That is what your Parliament suggested,
Majesty.

GEORGE	They did? They're not as stupid as I thought.
D'EON	Unfortunately, that would be a terrible mistake.
GEORGE	Perhaps for you. You couldn't mount an invasion then, could you. But from where I'm sitting—in the *victor's* chair—it seems a pretty fair deal.
D'EON	I do not speak solely of French interests here, Majesty. It is not a good idea from a British perspective as well.
GEORGE	Explain.
D'EON	(*signals to a clerk who gives GEORGE a packet of papers*) Dunkirk is an ideal port of trade for our two countries. I have prepared an extensive paper on this subject.
GEORGE	(*Toying with the paper, he ponders.*) I am impressed, d'Eon. Very impressed. What's next on the agenda?
D'EON	(*whispers*) Your Majesty will be happy to hear that a new shipment has arrived.
GEORGE	Ah! The Burgundy?
D'EON	Ten *barriques* of *vin rouge de Beaune* from my own private stock. Shall I put his Majesty down for... say... all of them?
GEORGE	Excellent, d'Eon! You are a wonderful diplomat... but you are an even better bootlegger.

> *D'EON bows. A light change. A fast transition to the French embassy. D'EON receives the Croix St. Louis from a member of the Secret. He pins it to his breast with great pride and marches downstage to a table with a lit candle and a bottle of wine – a* Pinot Noir.

He holds the candle behind the bottle and eyes the fine vintage. The Comte de GUERCHY is heard arguing outside with servants.

GUERCHY   Where is he?! Where is the upstart?!

SERVANT enters with GUERCHY and VERGY hot on his heels.

SERVANT   Comte de Guerchy with *attaché*.

GUERCHY   Ah ha! I suspected I'd find you here guzzling wine.

D'EON   My good Comte, the question of Burgundian wine is a subject as important as the business of nations.

GUERCHY   But wine isn't so important when it comes time to pay the bill, eh? Then you always manage to slip out the back door.

VERGY   We must compliment you, d'Eon. It's a fine little smuggling operation you have running through the embassy.

GUERCHY   That's right! Running through *my* embassy. You are shipping in so much wine that the British threaten to impose taxes on it!

D'EON   Forgive me, Comte Guerchy. I forgot to formally welcome you to England.

GUERCHY   What's that piece of tin on your breast?!

D'EON   The Croix Saint Louis. A reward from our King for my service here in England.

GUERCHY   Rubbish! What soldier's corpse did you steal it from?

D'EON   Perhaps you'd care to join me in a glass of...

GUERCHY   2,800 bottles charged to the King's coffers. Another invoice for an extra 1,800 bottles of prime Burgundy in one month alone. And not just *vin ordinaire* mind you – only the best. Do you think that the King... ye gods... take over for me, Vergy. I'm about to pop my valve.

VERGY   With pleasure, excellency. d'Eon, do you think the King is made of money?

D'EON   What do you expect from me? I am fulfilling my King's wishes. To do that I must cultivate a lifestyle that wins friends amongst our British hosts. Such diplomacy requires spending a good deal of money on my social life.

VERGY   And what a lavish social life you have. Cooks, servants, coachmen. You host elaborate parties and masquerades. You've only been here nine months and yet you've accumulated a tremendous debt.

D'EON   And what of France's debt to me? I have never been paid for my expenditures in Russia. I am afforded a pittance here by the Ministry of Finance. I am worth every penny that I have invoiced his Majesty.

VERGY   You're starting to talk treason.

D'EON   I am the acting ambassador.

GUERCHY   Not any more. I have new orders from Louis. (*He shows them.*) You are now my secretary. Perhaps you'd like to show some respect to your superior.

D'EON   (*He puts his hand on his sword.*) I have never been treated so shamefully.

VERGY moves to protect GUERCHY.

GUERCHY   You shall move from my official residence immediately. You shall find lodgings for yourself. You shall pay the rent with your own funds.

D'EON   You won't get away with this. (*storms out*)

GUERCHY   I already have.

He tastes D'EON's wine and is pleasantly surprised with its quality. Light change to a shadowy place. A member of the King's Secret chorus enters. He wears a grotesque two-faced mask. D'EON bursts into the scene in a rage.

SECRET 1   (*holding up a pomegranate*) I am the mouth of Broglie. Speak to me as you would to him.

BROGLIE appears on the opposite side of the stage. He speaks from France.

D'EON   What am I to do, Charles. Everything is falling to pieces.

BROGLIE   Calm yourself. Be more flexible and more reasonable.

D'EON   They seek to provoke me.

BROGLIE   You are not free to give yourself up to emotional outbursts. Take care that you do not embroil yourself. You must not fail the King.

D'EON   It is now a question of honour.

BROGLIE   Honour doesn't come into this. You are a spy. Stick to politics. If you go for honour, I am telling you, my friend, you will be sorry.

D'EON   Politics is a fickle whore that changes with each change of a minister. I am fed up with it. I choose honour.

BROGLIE   Know who you are dealing with. Guerchy will not take the course of honour.

D'EON   I have a long fuse, Charles, but that fuse is now at its end. Heaven help those who are caught in the blast! (*He exits.*)

> *BROGLIE and LOUIS XV confer on opposite sides of the stage. The MACARONI Brothers stand centre-stage.*

MACARONI 1   (*bows*) Brother Macaroni.

MACARONI 2   (*bows*) My dearest Macaroni.

MACARONI 1   Have you heard about d'Eon?

LOUIS   What has happened to d'Eon?

MACARONI 2   He has gone mad.

BROGLIE   He is completely out of my control.

LOUIS   Well, he has my papers! I want them back!

MACARONI 1   They say d'Eon tears his hair out.

MACARONI 2   I would too with Guerchy for a boss.

LOUIS   If they should fall into British hands, they'll know of my invasion.

BROGLIE   Your Majesty would do well not to provoke him.

MACARONI 1   They say the King will soon recall him for his impertinence.

MACARONI 2   Scandal!

BROGLIE   If your Majesty intercedes, he will run into the arms of British court.

LOUIS   He must be stopped. Recall him!

MACARONI 1	They say Louis is warming up a cell for him in the Bastille.
MACARONI 2	If the men from Bedlam don't grab him first!
	Both laugh identically.
	Light change to a diplomatic party. A confrontation between GUERCHY and D'EON.
GUERCHY	You will return the King's private letters immediately.
D'EON	I will not release them.
GUERCHY	This is not a request. If you don't then I will have Vergy tear your house apart.
D'EON	I wish him luck trying to find them.
GUERCHY	Do you recognize the seal on the document I hold.
D'EON	Yes.
GUERCHY	It is a direct order from our King. You are recalled to Versailles at once.
D'EON	I refuse to return to France.
GUERCHY	Then you go directly against the orders of your sovereign.
D'EON	I am not on French soil now. I am subject to Britain's laws. I never thought I would see the day when a foreign country would grant me the freedom denied me by my beloved France.
GUERCHY	You are a traitor then. Enjoy the dance.
	A collage of attempts on D'EON's life that takes the form of a dance in minuet. D'EON

> narrowly escapes stabbings, poison, crossbow, and strangling.

GUERCHY   He is impervious!

VERGY   I have searched his apartment.

GUERCHY   Did you find the King's papers?

VERGY   I found this. (*shows GUERCHY the portrait of POMPADOUR*)

GUERCHY   Our mistress?! Why would he have this?

VERGY   I can't imagine. He is a puzzle.

GUERCHY   A counter-spy? Blast him for being such a question-mark! Was he there when you searched?

VERGY   No. Gone to the country. But when he's in town the mob protects him. He rarely goes out without a guard.

GUERCHY   Then we are stymied again.

VERGY   Please, let me handle this, excellency. I believe that I have discovered his weak spot.

> *GUERCHY concedes and VERGY enters the dance. At some point he bumps into D'EON and everything stops.*

D'EON   My pardon, sir. The crowd presses close today.

VERGY   Do you not recognize me, d'Eon?

D'EON   Of course, Monsieur Vergy. You are secretary to the ambassador and a spy for Pompadour.

VERGY   And you are a spy for the Comte de Broglie – although one would never guess by your emasculate appearance.

D'EON   Your master has already tried to kidnap me, poison me with opium, stab me with daggers, and strangle me with the *garrote*. What makes you think that your petty insults will have any effect?

VERGY   Would you care for a pomegranate, d'Eon? They are in season now.

                D'EON is silent.

                By your reaction I take it that you would prefer some other fruit. Perhaps grapes would be more to your taste.

D'EON   I would prefer that you left my company.

VERGY   I'd offer you some grapes from your *terroirs* but they are so bitter. Hardly worth the effort to pick them.

D'EON   Their bitterness changes to divine sweetness when distilled.

VERGY   I have sampled your *Tonneroise*.

D'EON   They say that stolen wine tastes the best.

VERGY   Not in this case.

D'EON   If I valued your opinion, I might be insulted. You obviously know nothing of good wine.

VERGY   You are incorrect. I am from Chablis.

D'EON   Chablis is duck-piss.

VERGY   (*puts his hand slowly on his sword pommel*) ...I demand satisfaction.

D'EON   Name the time.

VERGY   Tomorrow morning at 5AM. Name the place.

D'EON	On the common at the edge of Golden Square. Weapons?
VERGY	Bring a saber and a second.
D'EON	With pleasure.

D'EON bows and exits. GUERCHY comes out of the shadows.

GUERCHY	Well done.
VERGY	Child's play.

A light change. Morning mist and the sound of night birds. D'EON and his second, John WILKES, wait for VERGY and party to arrive.

WILKES	Are you sure we are on the Common?
D'EON	Yes. This looks about right.
WILKES	I'm freezing.
D'EON	It'll warm up soon. You're very kind to do this, John.
WILKES	You have many friends in the British Court. I'm surprised you chose me.
D'EON	There are few I can trust like you.
WILKES	Why don't you call this off? You're on British soil now. French honour means nothing here.
D'EON	It will be over quickly.

The sound of horses. VERGY and entourage arrive. GUERCHY approaches WILKES.

GUERCHY	*(bows)* A very fresh morning, Mr. Wilkes.
WILKES	*(bows)* Delightful, Ambassador.

GUERCHY   For today, I abrogate my formal title. I am
            merely second to Monsieur Vergy. Have you
            brought your pistols?

WILKES   (*exchanging a glance with D'EON*) My associate
            was led to believe that we were to use sabers.

GUERCHY   My associate has had a change of heart. He
            chooses pistols.

WILKES   My associate has not brought pistols and
            would prefer the saber.

GUERCHY   Since my associate is the slighted one, he has
            the choice of weapon.

WILKES   This is true. But my associate has no pistol to
            duel with.

GUERCHY   An unfortunate dilemma... but one that
            can be easily resolved. My associate has
            brought an extra brace from his own
            private collection.

WILKES   I am afraid that would be highly irregular.

VERGY   Let's get on with it!

GUERCHY   Your associate may choose either pistol as a
            precaution against foul play.

            WILKES confers with D'EON.

VERGY   What's the matter, d'Eon? Are you worried
            that I'm a better shot than you are?

WILKES   We will continue.

            *The two braces are brought forward. D'EON
            chooses a pistol and starts to load.*

WILKES   The duellists will mark out four paces and
            face each other.

Both go to their positions.

GUERCHY   Call it in the air, d'Eon.

GUERCHY flips a sovereign.

D'EON   Crown.

GUERCHY   Crown it is. Monsieur d'Eon will shoot first.

D'EON   I would love to. But the firing mechanism on this gun has been tampered with.

WILKES rushes forward and checks.

VERGY   What a coincidence. So has mine.

He points it at D'EON and clicks the trigger.

...but these are fine...

Behind him, his entourage all pull pistols and point them at D'EON. VERGY steps back and GUERCHY steps forward.

D'EON   What is the meaning of this?

GUERCHY   This isn't a duel, d'Eon. It is an assassination.

GUERCHY aims but then a horn sounds. The sound of dogs. Enter Lord HALIFAX and SERVANT.

SERVANT   Prepare for the coming of His Lordship.

HALIFAX   What in George's name is going on here?! Who are these men, Sopwith?

SERVANT   I shall endeavour to find out, your Lordship. You men! My Lord wishes to know what you are doing on his land?

GUERCHY   His land? This is Golden Common.

HALIFAX   What's that? Why do they speak so strangely, Sopwith?

SERVANT   I believe they are of the French persuasion, your Lordship.

HALIFAX   Frenchies, hey! This is even more of an insult.

SERVANT   These gentlemen are under the impression that this is Golden Common.

HALIFAX   It most certainly is *not* Golden Common. Golden Common is beyond those trees. This is private property. Comprendo? And you Frenchies are *trespassing*, nest pass?

GUERCHY   d'Eon!

D'EON   (*bows*) Entirely my fault, Ambassador. I seem to have mistakenly brought us onto private land.

VERGY confers with the SERVANT.

SERVANT   Your Lordship, this would appear to be a matter of honour between these two...

D'EON   It most certainly is not. These men are assassins.

HALIFAX   What's that? Assassins? On my back lawn? What impudence! If you think I'm going to allow French blood to be spilled on my property—froggy blood on good, clean English soil—you have another think coming.

D'EON   You're Lordship is quite correct to point this out. May I offer my profoundest apologies?

HALIFAX   What's that?

SERVANT   This French gentleman wishes to apologize for their behaviour. Indeed, your Lordship. He seems to be the only gentleman in the lot. The rest all point pistols at us.

HALIFAX	So they do. So they do! Maybe you are looking for another war, eh? Maybe you'd like to have your pasty little froggy bottoms paddled all the way back to Versailles! Maybe you'd like to start by shooting the British Foreign Minister perhaps?!
VERGY	(*whispers to GUERCHY*) By god. It's Lord Halifax!
	GUERCHY signals – they drop their pistols reluctantly.
HALIFAX	That's better. You there. (*indicating D'EON*) You seem to be the only civilized one here. Come have some morning tea with me.
D'EON	I would be delighted, your Lordship.
HALIFAX	The rest of you rodents can bugger off my property!
	D'EON exits with a backward glance and sticks his tongue out at GUERCHY. GUERCHY is crippled with hatred. He descends to one knee as the scene changes to LOUIS and BROGLIE.
BROGLIE	He has printed a pamphlet.
LOUIS	Pamphlet? It is an encyclopedia of my secrets!
BROGLIE	He hasn't disclosed your invasion plans, Sire. You are safe for the moment.
LOUIS	He claims Guerchy tried to kill him. Christ, I wish he had.
BROGLIE	d'Eon is worth more to us alive.
LOUIS	He's a loose cannon.
BROGLIE	A loose cannon that is now the darling of the British court.

LOUIS	He refuses my orders!
BROGLIE	Outwardly, yes, Sire. But you must know that he still loves you and will die your faithful subject.
LOUIS	He is too dangerous.
BROGLIE	The more dangerous he becomes, the more valuable he is to us.

> *LOUIS ponders as GUERCHY and VERGY re-enter.*

VERGY	We are undone by this publication.
GUERCHY	Perhaps.
VERGY	It implicates us in a plot to murder him.
GUERCHY	What else?
VERGY	Well... nothing else. Isn't this enough? We are compromised.
GUERCHY	He's holding something back.
VERGY	Why aren't you listening to me? He has implicated us. To make matters worse, the British mobs back him. Some peasant just threw a rotten cabbage at my head. We must flee.
GUERCHY	We will not flee.
VERGY	I'm leaving for Paris in the morning.
GUERCHY	You will stay where you are! You will implicate us if you flee. What is this pamphlet but a bunch of scandalous lies.
VERGY	He has witnesses.
GUERCHY	(*scoffs*) John Wilkes – a rogue MP.

VERGY	And Lord Halifax.
GUERCHY	We must not panic. No. We will do the British thing. We will sue him for libel.

Light change in WILKES' house. D'EON, WILKES and CYNTHIA, a maid, confer.

WILKES	The bailiffs are on their way!
D'EON	Let's begin. Bring the dress.

CYNTHIA exits and re-enters with a servant's dress.

WILKES	Are you sure you want to do this?
D'EON	I will be recognized in my uniform. I must disguise myself.

D'EON takes the dress. CYNTHIA curtsies and exits.

WILKES	Yes, but the embarrassment.
D'EON	Momentary. Besides, I've seen you do it before.
WILKES	Yes, but only to sneak out of the House of Commons.

An expectant silence.

What are you waiting for?

D'EON	You must turn away.
WILKES	What?
D'EON	Turn away, John. I don't want you to see me change.
WILKES	Come, we haven't got time for games.

D'EON	I won't put it on unless you turn away.
WILKES	Oh, very well. How silly you are, d'Eon. A price on your head and you play peek-a-boo.
D'EON	(*undressing with his back to the audience*) It is a necessary precaution. I have hidden my true condition for so many years.
WILKES	What's that?
D'EON	My condition.
WILKES	What condition? Are you ill?
D'EON	No one must know, John. I only tell you because my escape demands it.
WILKES	I haven't got the foggiest idea what you are talking about.
D'EON	I've only told one other person in my life – and she didn't believe me either.
WILKES	Please hurry.
D'EON	She thought I was joking. But I wasn't. She's dead now. No one else knows.
WILKES	Knows what?
D'EON	John. Have you ever noticed how smooth my face is?
WILKES	Your face? Yes.
D'EON	That I have no Adam's apple?
WILKES	...well, one that's not pronounced.
D'EON	...and that I carry no shaving equipment? Have you noticed my breasts?
WILKES	You have a strong chest.

D'EON	Well then, here I am.

D'EON comes downstage in the dress as WILKES turns and is momentarily speechless.

WILKES	...by God. You look quite the part.
D'EON	I am the part.
WILKES	...you're...
D'EON	I am the part.
WILKES	That's not possible.
D'EON	I was raised as a man. My father needed a son to gain his inheritance.
WILKES	Lunacy.

The bailiffs pound and shout.

Christ! Let's go!

D'EON	Would you like to see my breasts?
WILKES	(*aghast*) No... no! You don't have to show me those. I believe you. Christ Jesus, I'm going to have to believe you. You could have chosen a more appropriate time to tell me about this!
D'EON	Please don't tell anyone.

Shouts. The sound of a door starting to give.

WILKES	You must hurry out the back. I'll hold them as long as I can.

Cynthia!

His maid re-enters.

CYNTHIA	Did he get away?

WILKES	Yes. There she is now, sneaking around from the back.
CYNTHIA	Fantastic! He's waltzed right past the bailiffs. He's a natural!
WILKES	Yes. Quite a natural.

> *WILKES whispers in CYNTHIA's ear. They exchange a glance. A light change. A gossip scene.*

CONTI	Say, have you heard about d'Eon?
MACARONI 1	What about him?
MACARONI 2	In a dress.
CONTI	To escape the bailiffs.
MACARONI 1	Just to escape? Or has he done it before?
CONTI	He seemed quite a natural.
MACARONI 2	Too natural.
CONTI	Wilkes commented on it.
MACARONI 1	On what?
CONTI	That he fit the part a little too well. But he was evasive.
MACARONI 2	So you think.
CONTI	I don't think anything.

> *CONTI exits. BROGLIE enters into the discussion.*

MACARONI 2	So, have you heard about d'Eon.
BROGLIE	What now?

MACARONI 1   His trial is soon.

BROGLIE   So I hear.

MACARONI 2   If this gets out in court.

BROGLIE   If what gets out?

MACARONI 2   This rumour.

MACARONI 1   What if they ask him on the stand?

BROGLIE   Ask him what?

MACARONI 1   You know. (*touches his nose*) What an embarrassment.

BROGLIE   Tell me.

> *MACARONI 1 whispers into BROGLIE's ear.*

A what?

MACARONI 2   A woman!

BROGLIE   A...

MACARONI 2   Yes! Think of the *scandal*!

> *MACARONIS exit leaving BROGLIE alone onstage.*

BROGLIE   ...he said he loved me.

> *Light change. A courtroom scene.*

SERVANT   All rise for the Chief Justice, Lord Mansfield. Be upstanding! Court is now in session.

MANSFIELD   In the case of Mister d'Eon's pamphlet *Lettres, mémoires, et négociations*. I find the defendant gu...

D'EON	My lord! I am here to defend myself in the final hour.
MANSFIELD	I am glad the defendant finally took time from his busy schedule to grace this court with his presence.
D'EON	My Lord, my absence was not out of disrespect for your court. I have feared for my life all this time.
MANSFIELD	Whatever. Do you have any final comments?
D'EON	Only that I am innocent of these charges. My pamphlet was an embarrassment to the French diplomatic community. But since when is embarrassing a bunch of French bureaucrats a crime in a British court of law? Were I in my own country, I would most certainly be thrown into the Bastille. But the course of French justice is skewed by unfair rules of privilege. As a Frenchman, I am ashamed to admit that France's laws are not as judicious as My Lord's English laws.
MANSFIELD	Well, of course. This is self-evident. The basis of all British laws is Liberty!

> *GUERCHY snorts and gets an evil look from MANSFIELD.*

D'EON	Secondly, I have not been formally arrested.
GUERCHY	Only because you ducked the bailiffs!
MANSFIELD	Silence! Pray continue, Mister d'Eon.
D'EON	I throw myself at the mercy of the court.
LAWYER	May I remind mi'lud, of this man's libel of my two clients.
MANSFIELD	What have you to say to this?

D'EON	Only that it is not libel, but pure truth, my Lord.
GUERCHY	There you have it! He repeats his filthy slurs in a court of law!
MANSFIELD	*Silence*! One more word from you Mister Guerchy and I will toss you across the Channel. I grow exceedingly impatient that internal French matters are tying up this British courtroom.
LAWYER	All the more reason to extradite him, mi'lud.
MANSFIELD	Hmph. (*to* VERGY) What about you, sir? You've sat silent as a clam at low tide throughout this whole sordid affair. Do you have anything to say?

VERGY shakes his head.

Does he have trouble speaking English, counsel?

LAWYER	...his English is excellent, mi'lud.
MANSFIELD	Then let him speak. I want to hear these charges come from his own mouth.
VERGY	...I...
GUERCHY	(*whispers*) Don't say a word.
MANSFIELD	Don't let this bully shut you up! You are free to speak here, Mister Vergy. This is England.
VERGY	d'Eon... speaks the truth.

All gasp! GUERCHY is apoplectic.

I have been part of a conspiracy to murder him – a plot ordered by the Comte de Guerchy.

GUERCHY   You moron!

VERGY   My Christian conscience prevents me from
                 lying any further. May God forgive me!
                 (*crosses himself*)

GUERCHY   I'll ring your Christian neck!

                     GUERCHY tries to strangle VERGY.
                     Pandemonium.

MANSFIELD   Come to order! Separate those two! Well, this
                 is a first. They say that "truth will out" but
                 I've rarely experienced that in my own
                 courtroom. What more is there to say? Mister
                 d'Eon, you are a free man. Should you wish
                 to press charges against these two men, I
                 would be happy to accept your indictment.

                     D'EON bows deeply. A light change. He is
                     triumphant. LOUIS and BROGLIE enter.

LOUIS   He wants how much?!

BROGLIE   300,000 livres, Majesty, and reinstatement as
                 Plenipotentiary Ambassador.

LOUIS   And if I don't agree?

BROGLIE   He will publish your invasion plans.

LOUIS   So it's blackmail!

BROGLIE   No, Sire. He only seeks to regain what he has
                 lost.

LOUIS   You continue to defend him even though he
                 hurls mud at me from across the channel.

BROGLIE   He is entrenched within the British court. He
                 is still your loyal spy, Sire.

LOUIS   He's a popinjay!

BROGLIE   There is something else, Sire.

LOUIS   What more damage can this man do!?

BROGLIE   There are rumours starting, Sire. About d'Eon.

LOUIS   What kind of rumours?

BROGLIE   They question his sex.

LOUIS   His what?

BROGLIE   His sex, sire, his sex... "S"... "E"...

LOUIS   I know what sex is, damn you! What are they saying?

BROGLIE   That he is a woman.

LOUIS   ...really?

BROGLIE   Disguised since birth to obtain an inheritance.

LOUIS   But... you fought with him.

BROGLIE   I never once saw him shave.

LOUIS   Twaddle. Have you seen his sword arm? It's like an oak. He is a man in every respect.

BROGLIE   Possibly, Sire. The rumours come from many sources. They are even starting to take bets in a London coffee-house called "Lloyds".

LOUIS   Astounding. Has he admitted it himself?

BROGLIE   He has not denied it.

LOUIS   This sets everything askew.

BROGLIE   Why, Sire?

LOUIS	Because we can't have a bloody woman skulking around as one of our spies! We'd be the laughing stock of Europe.
BROGLIE	Since when has your Majesty prevented women from assuming roles of...
LOUIS	Hold your tongue. My dearest Pompadour is dead now. You won't dirty her name. I wonder what she'd do with this news?
BROGLIE	I will not insult her dead name by providing an answer, Sire.
LOUIS	Leave me.

BROGLIE exits.

Everyone is against me. My own ministers make fun of me now that Pompadour is gone – how I miss her tight little arse. The British laugh at me! What right have they to laugh? I am supreme in my own country not bound by some stupid Parliament filled with sheep-farming upstarts! My will is God's will. I *am* *Louis Quinze!* All bow for the coming of His Royal Majesty King Louis the Fifteenth, Supreme Ruler of all France, Grande Overseer of the Colonies of North America, Rightful and Legitimate Heir of Louis Fourteen Sun King, Commander General of all French Forces, World Conqueror... Royal Countenance Unsurpassed... Radiant Visage... He Alone Blessed by God...

He collapses.

SERVANT	The King is *dead*! Long live our new King, Louis XVI!

A party. All cheer the passing of LOUIS XV. A pair of masked men piss on the old King's corpse as LOUIS XVI is carried onto the stage in triumph. He struts forward confidently, BROGLIE bows before him.

LOUIS XVI   (*signals BROGLIE*) You are fired. But before you go, I have some final orders for you. Call back all the ambassadors. Destroy all compromising files. Disband the King's Secret... and bring me the head of the Chevalier d'Eon.

Blackout.

ACT TWO

*A fashion show for LOUIS XVI put on by
Rose BERTIN and the MACARONI brothers.
They speak through fashionable megaphones
as models parade in front of the King.*

MACARONI 1   Everyone is doing it!

MACARONI 2   Let's do it!

BOTH   Let's push the fashion envelope!

A model enters.

MACARONI 1   From la Maison Bertin, here is Alphonse in a startling little number.

MACARONI 2   Note the buckles and white-lace!

MACARONI 1   What a pretty little picture. He is sure to turn heads at this year's Cotillion.

Another model struts by.

MACARONI 1   Georges is ready for a night out on the town...

MACARONI 2   The diamond studded brocade bounces off his jacket in a perfect cascade and spills onto blackened pantaloon. See how his sword cane cuts a dashing pace...

MACARONI 1   What a triumph!

MACARONI 2   And now...

MACARONI 1   For the ultimate fashion risk...

MACARONI 2   Here comes... Elene in a stunning demi-dress...

A model enters in a costume that is half-dress and half-soldier's uniform.

MACARONI 1   Qu'elle surprise!

LOUIS XVI   (*standing*) This is an outrage!

MACARONI 2   From Madame Bertin's personal design, Sire. In honour of the celebrated Chevaliere. It will be all the rage this season.

LOUIS XVI   That's the Croix Saint-Louis on its breast!

MACARONI 2   Only a fake, sire. A copy of d'Eon's original.

LOUIS XVI   This is a violation!

MACARONI 1   You have offended his Majesty.

MACARONI 2   Me? It was *you* who chose the swatches for Madame Bertin.

MACARONI 1   That's right. Blame me. It's always my fault.

MACARONI 2   Why not? If the slipper fits...

LOUIS XVI   Bertin! Where the hell are you?

BERTIN   (*offstage*) What is the problem now?

LOUIS XVI   What crap are you designing here? How dare you.

BERTIN   What's the problem, Majesty?

LOUIS XVI   I absolutely forbid anyone to wear this abomination. Destroy it immediately.

BERTIN   Why?

LOUIS XVI   We will not encourage a celebration of freaks.

BERTIN   My designs only reflect popular sentiment. It's what the people want.

MACARONI 1   Yes! That's right. It's what we want!

MACARONI 2	The people have spoken!
LOUIS XVI	Get out of here, you stupid Macaronis!
	They scurry away.
BERTIN	Your wife approved the design.
LOUIS XVI	Then you are saved by her influence once again, Bertin. Back to your Atelier. And take that rag with you!
BERTIN	At once, sire. (*bows and exits*)
LOUIS XVI	What a disaster. I am surrounded by deviates and provocateurs. All right. Who's next on the agenda?
BEAUMARCHAIS	An entreaty, Sire. From the playwright, Pierre-Augustin Caron de Beaumarchais!
	Spontaneous and extended applause as BEAUMARCHAIS enters triumphant. LOUIS XVI claps as well.
BEAUMARCHAIS	Please, your Majesty grants me too much honour.
LOUIS XVI	Nonsense, Beaumarchais. Everyone is right to clap. Paris is abuzz with your accomplishments.
BEAUMARCHAIS	Only with the gracious patronage of your Majesty.
LOUIS XVI	When does your new thing open at *la Comedie*?
BEAUMARCHAIS	"*Thing*?" My *Barber of Seville* opens Tuesday night!
LOUIS XVI	Well, you must be very excited.

BEAUMARCHAIS   Yes, Majesty. But there are some problems. The Royal censors are seeking revisions.

LOUIS XVI   Revisions?

BEAUMARCHAIS   ...yes... that will compromise the very nature of the text.

LOUIS XVI   Well, go on. Tell me what the problem is.

BEAUMARCHAIS   This is most embarrassing, Sire. They seek to... to water down the actions of some of the characters.

LOUIS XVI   Which characters?

BEAUMARCHAIS   ...the nobility... characters who must take the fall for the comedy of the piece to succeed.

LOUIS XVI   You are making fun of the nobility?

BEAUMARCHAIS   No, Sire. Never. Just the particular actions of a certain nobleman – a pompous creature, Sire. Worthy of ridicule.

LOUIS XVI   You are saying that the nobility of France is pompous?

BEAUMARCHAIS   Never, Sire. But... surely you yourself can think of a few examples of pompous men of privilege – even in your own court.

LOUIS XVI   Me? In my own court? Let's see. I can't say that I do. All the nobles of my court have been most humble to me.

The nobles make fawning noises.

BEAUMARCHAIS   Well, naturally, Sire.

LOUIS XVI   I think perhaps your own speedy ascension through the ranks of the middle-class has coloured your opinion. What you perceive as pompousness is merely... detachment from the commonality of everyday life. I am loathe to say it, but the censors are right to rebuke you.

BEAUMARCHAIS But...

LOUIS XVI The wealthy are so embattled these days. What sort of impression do we give the lower classes if you slap nobility in the face on the King's stage?

BEAUMARCHAIS ...I am compromised.

LOUIS XVI (*ponders*) Yes, I can see that. This will never do. We would never presume to block your creative vision. Is that the correct theatrical term?

> *BEAUMARCHAIS nods.*

You needn't worry, Beaumarchais. I will have someone talk to the censors.

BEAUMARCHAIS His Majesty is most gracious.

LOUIS XVI But in return...

BEAUMARCHAIS Return?

LOUIS XVI Of course. You are most certainly in the wrong about this. I stick my neck out for you – so you must perform a service for me.

BEAUMARCHAIS (*kneels*) I am at your disposal.

LOUIS XVI You are to proceed at once to London.

BEAUMARCHAIS Immediately?

LOUIS XVI Yes.

BEAUMARCHAIS But... I'll miss my opening.

LOUIS XVI So what? It's just a stupid play. When you have reached London you will meet with the Chevalier d'Eon de Beaumont.

BEAUMARCHAIS The woman?

LOUIS XVI Yes, the woman. You will demand that she return immediately to my court. You will not return from England without her.

BEAUMARCHAIS Everything I have read about this remarkable lady would indicate that she is most contrary to the wishes of this court.

LOUIS XVI I had hoped to have her head on display in Paris as a lesson to the mob.

BEAUMARCHAIS Respectfully, were she a man, this would be appropriate action. But she is not and so requires a more delicate approach.

LOUIS XVI It'll be bribery then. I hear she is near destitute. My clerks will draw up a deal. When it's ready you will proceed to London and present it to her. If she accepts quickly, then perhaps you will be able to return in time to catch the second performance of your play.

BEAUMARCHAIS I hope to be back sooner. Second nights are notoriously dull.

LOUIS XVI Dull? One of your charming little skits? Never!

Light change. D'EON's library/study in London. He waits anxiously for Jean-Jacques ROUSSEAU. MORANDE enters.

D'EON Morande, is he here?

MORANDE Monsieur Jean-Jacques Rousseau. (*He exits.*)

> *ROUSSEAU enters and D'EON kneels at his feet.*

D'EON Master. Had I known you were in London I would have invited you to my humble house much sooner.

ROUSSEAU Chevalier, there is no need to kneel before me.

D'EON You are my master. Master in philosophy, in literature and in letters.

ROUSSEAU You have become quite a man of letters yourself. I have enjoyed our correspondence. Arise. I am pleased to meet the flesh behind the pen.

D'EON Welcome to my house.

ROUSSEAU I confess that my main purpose in this visit is purely selfish. I want a peek at this famous library of yours.

D'EON All I have is yours to study.

> *ROUSSEAU peruses D'EON's massive collection.*

ROUSSEAU Good. No doubt one of the best collections in England.

D'EON In all of Europe.

ROUSSEAU What's here? Herodotus!

D'EON Here's a personal favourite.

ROUSSEAU My god. Third Century! May I?

D'EON Of course. An illuminated text from Italy. An unparalleled encyclopedia of ancient races.

ROUSSEAU Let's see... "A" is for... Amazon! Fascinating.

D'EON	Yes.
ROUSSEAU	Quite extensive. But... some puzzlements as well.
D'EON	How so?
ROUSSEAU	Mary Astell... Marianne Faques. These are feminine writers.
D'EON	Yes.
ROUSSEAU	Your taste here is slightly offbeat, Monsieur.
D'EON	These are most insightful authors regarding issues of gender.

A silence.

ROUSSEAU	So what's this I hear about you being a woman?

MORANDE enters.

MORANDE	Your pardon, Sirs.
D'EON	What is it?
MORANDE	A Monsieur Beaumarchais to see you.
D'EON	Should I know him?
MORANDE	Pierre-Augustin Beaumarchais – the famous playwright.
D'EON	A playwright? Send him away.
MORANDE	He bears a letter from the King.
D'EON	I'm busy right now. Deal with him yourself.
MORANDE	Very good, Chevaliere. (*bows and exits*)
ROUSSEAU	Now where were we?

D'EON   We were talking about Herodotus.

ROUSSEAU   Don't play coy, *Chevalier-e*. Your name is on everyone's lips.

D'EON   I don't pay attention to the rumour mill.

ROUSSEAU   Even when it is you that they talk about? I'll ask you a second time. Are you a woman?

D'EON   Should it matter so much if I was?

ROUSSEAU   It matters a great deal to me. It would mean that our entire relationship—our friendship established through quite personal correspondence—is based upon a lie.

D'EON   Master, I do not understand.

ROUSSEAU   Look at all the problems facing France today. What is the primary cause of its decay?

D'EON   The royal family.

ROUSSEAU   Wrong! Wrong! It is *women*! Women are to blame! Pompadour, Sophia-Charlotte! By becoming power brokers in the public sphere, they have upset the natural balance. I am a new breed of thinker who believes that there is a moral and physical weakness in women that should prevent them from attaining the rank and power of a man.

D'EON   Why am I positive that this new breed of thinkers you speak of are all men?

ROUSSEAU   This is the Age of Reason. Women, by their irrational natures, are naturally excluded from reasoning. There are no good morals for women outside of a withdrawn and domestic life.

D'EON   What if women do not wish to stay at home?

ROUSSEAU	Quit evading the question!
D'EON	You don't ask any questions. You pontificate from atop that pole between your legs.
ROUSSEAU	I'll ask you a third time. Are you a woman?!
D'EON	...if I answer that I am?
ROUSSEAU	Then our meeting is concluded. I will wish you well and advise you to bear many children.
D'EON	And if I say that I am a man?
ROUSSEAU	Then our friendship may continue.
D'EON	I am a man then.
ROUSSEAU	That... is just the sort of answer I would expect from a woman.
D'EON	What would you have me say then?
ROUSSEAU	The truth!
D'EON	The truth is that I would like to change the subject.
ROUSSEAU	Quit talking in circles.
D'EON	That is the fate of all conversation.
ROUSSEAU	And who's fault is that? Women! You have ruined public discourse with your feminine ramblings!
D'EON	So, you assume that I am a woman.
ROUSSEAU	I assume nothing. You may merely be... an infected male.
D'EON	So perhaps I am a man after all.

ROUSSEAU	Yes. I think that you are a perfect product of the French court. A feminization of the aristocratic male. You suffer from "eviration." Too much sex with the whores in Louis' harem has reduced you to a half-man.
D'EON	Monsieur Rousseau, as a philosopher you are unparalleled. I bow to the genius of your Social Contract. But regarding the small matter of me, your theories are completely without substance.
ROUSSEAU	It is a scientific fact that too much sex with a woman permanently shrinks a man's member. This lessening of virility can only encourage a growth of a man's feminine side.
D'EON	You obviously never spent much time at Versailles. There, one could see the King's bloated penis on display at all times. I came upon it one day, poking out of one of the topiaries; it certainly didn't look shrunken to me and he fucked thousands of women. As to your accusations of my own promiscuity – here you are completely off the mark. I am a virgin.
ROUSSEAU	...a virgin?
D'EON	Yes.
ROUSSEAU	So you've never... (*makes a poking gesture*)
D'EON	Never.
ROUSSEAU	By choice.
D'EON	Entirely.

ROUSSEAU is silent.

You are baffled.

ROUSSEAU   I've never met a virgin-by-choice. I didn't
                think you existed anymore.

D'EON   Why not?

ROUSSEAU   Well... because everything comes down to the
                "act". Doesn't it with you?

                D'EON shakes his head.

                You don't think about "doing it" all the time?
                Sweet mercy, French society revolves around
                it.

D'EON   No.

ROUSSEAU   Hell, even I think about it – and I am – well,
                we won't get into that... and just about every
                other creature on the planet thinks about it!

                D'EON shrugs.

ROUSSEAU   What are you then?

D'EON   I am.

ROUSSEAU   I suppose it's not unprecedented. There was
                another. I mean... (*smirks*) the last French
                virgin-by-choice I can think of was... you
                know... Jeanne d'Arc. (*He laughs.*)

D'EON   Yes. (*laughs*) I am Jeanne d'Arc.

                *They both laugh but ROUSSEAU isn't clear
                about what is so funny.*

ROUSSEAU   Well, as they say in this country, it has been
                "a slice of cake" meeting you, but I really
                must be going...

D'EON   Just when our conversation was becoming so
                interesting.

ROUSSEAU   The King may not find it so. It was he who
            sent me. Adieu.

            *Bows and exits quickly. Light change.
            BEAUMARCHAIS and MORANDE sip
            coffee in Lloyds. Behind them bookies take
            silent bets and draw odds on the wall.*

MORANDE   She will not see you.

BEAUMARCHAIS   I bear orders from the King.

MORANDE   She doesn't care.

BEAUMARCHAIS   Morande, you are close to this woman.

MORANDE   Yes. She gave me this locket.

BEAUMARCHAIS   Give it to me.

            MORANDE hands it over reluctantly.

BEAUMARCHAIS   You know d'Eon is heading for the old
            chop-chop.

MORANDE   That is precisely why she won't go back to
            France with you.

BEAUMARCHAIS   What about you, Morande? Do you feel safe
            here?

MORANDE   I understand how far the King's hand can
            stretch. d'Eon has been very lucky so far.

BEAUMARCHAIS   She would appear to have a significant
            supply of horseshoes up her arse. Morande...
            how would you like an official pardon?

MORANDE   That would depend. May I have d'Eon's
            locket back?

BEAUMARCHAIS   No. I have a use for it.

MORANDE	...I must be allowed to continue publishing my *Gazetier*.
BEAUMARCHAIS	I can't guarantee that.
MORANDE	No deal then.
BEAUMARCHAIS	But I would solicit the King directly.
MORANDE	What else do you offer?
BEAUMARCHAIS	Safe conduct. 30,000 livres. Your papers renewed. No mention to your rival publishers of your taste for pornographic poetry.
MORANDE	...in exchange for what?
BEAUMARCHAIS	Help me with d'Eon. Lure her out of the house. I'll do the rest.
MORANDE	She's wise to kidnapping ploys.
BEAUMARCHAIS	Ask her out for a drink. How difficult can that be?
MORANDE	Very. She never leaves the apartment without a heavy compliment of supporters. She's locked in tighter than a crab up the arse of a Montmartre whore.
BEAUMARCHAIS	Colourful imagery.
MORANDE	Thank you.
BEAUMARCHAIS	(*standing*) Well, it appears that if I am to make my Paris opening, I'm going to have to do everything myself.
MORANDE	Impossible.
BEAUMARCHAIS	Watch and learn. If I cannot go to her, then she must come to me.

He beckons the bookies.

	Gentlemen. What odds are you taking currently regarding the sex of the Chevalier d'Eon?
BOOKIE 1	Currently 3 to 2 that he is a man.
BEAUMARCHAIS	I'll wager 3 to 1 odds that she is a woman.
BOOKIE 2	That's poor odds for you. Why are you so confident?
BEAUMARCHAIS	(*shrugs*) I'm French. I'm stupid.
BOOKIE 3	How much will you wager at 3 to 1?
BEAUMARCHAIS	I'm so new at this. 10,000 livres?
BOOKIE 1	What's that here? Two pounds?

General laughter.

BEAUMARCHAIS	Forgive me. I forgot I was in England. Five-hundred pounds.

Shocked silence.

BOOKIE 1	Five-hundred?
BEAUMARCHAIS	Too low? One thousand pounds... at 4 to 1!

Pandemonium. BOOKIE 1 silences everyone.

BOOKIE 1	We want to know what you know.
BEAUMARCHAIS	Add another thousand pounds to my wager then. Two thousand pounds.

All gasp!

BOOKIE 1	Tell us or we won't take your bet.
BEAUMARCHAIS	Very well. This letter is from the King of France. It is proof positive of d'Eon's sex. Louis XVI has known all along. The King

orders her to quit the façade, don the clothes of her true sex, and return to France dressed as a woman.

MORANDE   (*aside*) How do you know that this will work?

BEAUMARCHAIS   Does she read the papers?

MORANDE   Yes.

BEAUMARCHAIS   It'll work.

BOOKIE 2   Let us see it.

BEAUMARCHAIS   Ah! It is sealed with the King's mark. Only d'Eon may open it. Bring d'Eon here and you will have your answer.

The BOOKIES confer to the side.

BOOKIE 2   Can this be true?

BOOKIE 3   What's the count?

BOOKIE 1   Bets for and against have reached 60,000 pounds.

BEAUMARCHAIS   (*stepping within earshot of the bookies*) You know, Morande. They say that d'Eon had his stockbroker take out 5,000 pounds on his being a woman.

BOOKIE 1   (*whispers*) 5,000 pounds!

MORANDE   It's obvious he's been in on it from the start. He'll take us all to the cleaners.

BOOKIE 2   (*whispers*) He'll take us to the cleaners!

BEAUMARCHAIS & MORANDE   What a crook!

ALL BOOKIES   What a crook!

BOOKIE 3   I'm taking odds at 6 to 1 that he is a she!

                  A cheer. Light change. BEAUMARCHAIS
                  and MORANDE look at their watches.

MORANDE   You haven't much time.

BEAUMARCHAIS   In my previous life I was a watchmaker. Time
                  is always on my side.

                  Light change. He takes out D'EON's locket
                  and twirls it.

                  Another five hundred pounds at ten to one.

BOOKIE 1   What collateral do you have?

BEAUMARCHAIS   This golden locket.

BOOKIE 1   It can't be worth more than twenty.

BEAUMARCHAIS   The lady in question gave it to me as a
                  personal gift.

BOOKIE 2   Let us see the inscription.

BEAUMARCHAIS   Certainly.

                  He hands it over and then checks his pocket
                  watch.

BOOKIE 2   "With undying devotion, the Chevaliere
                  d'Eon de Beaumont."

BEAUMARCHAIS   We are lovers.

                  All gasp!

                  And I intend to marry her. Three-two-one-
                  eh...

                  D'EON appears in a fury.

D'EON   Where is that fucking playwright?!

BEAUMARCHAIS   Darling. Such language.

D'EON   This pathetic display has gone on long
enough. What sort of a twisted individual are
you? I refuse to see you so you try to slander
my good name.

BEAUMARCHAIS   "Good" name? I wasn't aware you had one of
those.

D'EON   (*to all*) This man is a liar. I have not wagered
in this affair. That is a lie. I am not engaged to
this man. That is a lie as well. I don't give a
damn whether you swindle each other out of
your dirty fortunes. Just don't drag me down
with you!

BEAUMARCHAIS   Too late.

D'EON   (*approaches him*) I wouldn't expect someone
who frequents this den of thieves to know
anything about honour.

BEAUMARCHAIS   Oh really? I possess just as much honour as
the next man.

D'EON   Do you?

BEAUMARCHAIS   For what that's worth.

D'EON   (*slaps him*) Then we will duel right here and
now.

BOOKIE 1   Two to one for d'Eon!

      Clamour.

D'EON   Silence, you maggots!

BEAUMARCHAIS   d'Eon. I would love to pop those dragoon
buttons of yours with my epee. But I am
afraid that I am unable to comply.

D'EON   Then you are an honourless coward.

BEAUMARCHAIS Far from it. Were you a man, I would happily stick you like a pin-cushion, but what would people say? Me fighting a defenseless woman? You *are* a woman – aren't you?

> *All gaze intently at him. D'EON realizes that a fortune hangs in the balance of his reply. The BOOKIES start to close in on him.*

Things are a getting a little close in here. You'd better come with me if you don't want your pants ripped off by these vultures.

> *A light change. They speak alone.*

(*pats his forehead with a kerchief*) That was a close thing, eh?

D'EON I despise you.

BEAUMARCHAIS Join the critics. (*looks at his watch*) Now be a good chap and let's catch a fast sloop back to France. With luck you and I should just make the curtain for Act II. I have box seats.

D'EON You know my answer to that.

BEAUMARCHAIS You must flee with me. They'll soon gather courage in there and come looking for you. I'm afraid your life here in England isn't worth much any more.

MORANDE He's right, d'Eon.

D'EON You're in on this as well?

> *MORANDE nods.*

BEAUMARCHAIS He had to. I blackmailed him. Shall we read you the King's offer?

> *D'EON nods reluctantly.*

(*tosses it to MORANDE*) You read it, Morande. Make yourself useful.

> *MORANDE breaks the seal.*

LOUIS XVI (*speaks from a separate area of the stage*) In compensation for the services that the Chevaliere d'Eon has rendered in Russia and England as well as in my armies and other commissions that were promised to her, I gladly want to assure her an annual pension of 12,000 livres. This I will pay to her exactly but only upon her safe return to my shores dressed in the natural garb of her gender.

BEAUMARCHAIS So you see. All this fuss was for nothing. (*bows in mock reverence*) You are not an outcast. You are a heroine. Return to France with me and accept your laurels and pretty frocks with graciousness.

> *He offers his hand. D'EON takes it reluctantly.*

D'EON Beaumarchais.

BEAUMARCHAIS Oui, Mademoiselle?

D'EON ...Merde.

BEAUMARCHAIS (*kissing D'EON's hand*) Merci milles fois.

> *Light change. The Atelier of Madame BERTIN.*

ASSISTANT She is ready!

BERTIN I am unprepared. Let her wait.

ASSISTANT Is that wise, Madame?

BERTIN Duchess, Chevaliere, Contessa – their titles mean nothing. I take out my little stick and slap them hard on their flabby thighs if they try to conceal their fat. They know that my little stick misses nothing. They must all inevitably bow down and measure up to Rose Bertin.

ASSISTANT   Madame rules them all like a Queen!

BERTIN   Babette, that is so true. I am the sovereign of their skirts. And I am now ready to discover this one's secrets. Send her in.

> *ASSISTANT curtsies and exits. D'EON enters in a half-finished dress.*

BERTIN   (*curtsies*) Mademoiselle, you are a vision.

D'EON   A vision of unhappiness.

BERTIN   Well, naturally. The dress isn't finished. And the fit may be slightly off. The result of you having sent me your measurements by post.

D'EON   Do you suggest that I would be dishonest about my size and shape?

BERTIN   Never, Mademoiselle. But a personal measurement is so much better.

D'EON   I suppose.

BERTIN   So you will allow me?

> *D'EON nods approval. BERTIN approaches D'EON with her stick.*

BERTIN   You have a charming leg, Mademoiselle.

D'EON   Thank you.

BERTIN   *Quarante.* (*outer leg*)

ASSISTANT   *Quarante.*

D'EON	Will I be ready for the King's party, do you think?
BERTIN	Well, I don't know about you but the dress certainly shall be. (*chuckles*) *Vingt-trois.* (*arm*)
ASSISTANT	*Vingt-trois.*
BERTIN	You must be very excited.
D'EON	I have been to Versailles before.
BERTIN	But this time under such unusual circumstances.
D'EON	Yes.
BERTIN	All eyes will be upon you.
D'EON	I have grown used to that.
BERTIN	*Quarante-trois.* (*chest*)
ASSISTANT	*Quarante-trois.*
BERTIN	You will hike your skirts now.
D'EON	Why?
BERTIN	So that I may measure your crotch.
D'EON	Why would a dressmaker wish to measure my crotch?
BERTIN	...good question. I will measure your in seam then.
D'EON	I will lift my dress.
BERTIN	You will hold the stick here, Mademoiselle.
D'EON	I am not a nervous debutante, Madame Bertin. You may place your stick wherever you please.

BERTIN   Very well.

D'EON   You are naturally curious.

BERTIN   Half of Europe is. *Trent.*

ASSISTANT   *Trent.*

D'EON   I will disrobe if you prefer.

BERTIN   That will not be necessary. C'est finis, Mademoiselle. Do you feel better now?

D'EON   I am still unhappy.

BERTIN   How can this be? I have never designed a blue satin more beautiful than this. You'll make me cry if you continue.

D'EON   I do not wish to wear a dress.

BERTIN   You'd rather parade about in that dusty old Dragoon's costume of yours.

D'EON   I prefer to dress in uniform.

BERTIN   (*whispers to ASSISTANT*) It seems that we must take a more military approach with Mademoiselle. d'Eon! Stand up straight!

   D'EON straightens up.

BERTIN   You are a soldier! You must obey the order of your commander in chief. Yes?

D'EON   Yes.

BERTIN   A maiden in Dragoon red! What commander would allow that?

D'EON   You speak with such certainty... but this dress... I dare not look at myself in the mirror.

BERTIN	Be quiet, you quivering jelly! Hmph. Some soldier here. Scared of her own reflection!
D'EON	I am ashamed.
BERTIN	Gather courage! Consider this to be your crossing of the Rubicon. On one shore is your false life as a man, on the other, your true life as a woman. Obey your orders, Captain. Make the crossing! (*salutes*)
D'EON	I obey. (*salutes*)
BERTIN	Thank you for your patience, Mademoiselle. May I say what a pleasure it is for me to have you to wear one of my creations.

BERTIN curtsies as D'EON exits.

ASSISTANT	Well?
BERTIN	Definitely... a woman!
ASSISTANT	(*jumping up and down and clapping*) *Merveilleux!*
BERTIN	Score one for our sex. Yes! (*She pumps her arm in victory.*)

Lighting change. An opulent party given by LOUIS XVI. A courtly dance. D'EON is swept forward to greet the King and Marie-ANTOINETTE.

LOUIS XVI	Come here, d'Eon! You must think I've been hiding from you all evening.
D'EON	Not at all, Majesty.
LOUIS XVI	Perhaps that would be the proper thing though, given your uncanny resemblance to *la pucelle*. Perhaps I should pretend to be a simple nobleman and seek to fool you!

D'EON   I have never encouraged such comparisons, Majesty. I am a simple soldier.

LOUIS XVI   Not anymore you aren't. You are now one of our brightest feminine lights in the French sky! Have you met my little Austrian crumpet?

D'EON   *Guten aben*, Majesty.

ANTOINETTE   What a funny accent you have!

D'EON   Yes. Very funny.

ANTOINETTE   How does Mademoiselle d'Eon find her new uniform?

D'EON   Madame, I am pleased to wear it because it admits me to the Regiment of the Queen, which in all times and in all places is totally devoted to the service of our good King.

LOUIS XVI   Ha ha! Two flatteries in one! Very good!

ANTOINETTE   Mademoiselle, if the regiment was composed of only demoiselles, who but d'Eon could command it?

D'EON   Madame, it would rather be Marie-Antoinette of Austria.

LOUIS XVI   Ah ha! Check-mate!

ANTOINETTE   Mademoiselle, the King has given you a good pension from his royal treasury, and as for myself, I will now give you more...

LOUIS XVI   Here now. Steady on.

ANTOINETTE   Dearest husband, go start a war somewhere and leave us alone.

LOUIS XVI   Do you know what they call my little Austrian flower around here, d'Eon? Madame *le Deficit*.

ANTOINETTE	They hate me.
LOUIS XVI	Never, dear. They all love you here. (*claps his hands to all present and shouts*) Doesn't everyone here just *love* the Queen?!
	A few non-committal grunts.
	They just don't like your expensive tastes, dear.
ANTOINETTE	They hate me because I'm not French! But here, we insult our guest by bickering. Let's get back to the subject at hand. Mademoiselle, the first ladies of the court will show you how to wear Madame Bertin's dresses with suitable decency until such time as we can find a Versailles household where your instruction can be perfected.
D'EON	I thank you, Madame. (*curtsies*)
LOUIS XVI	Are you two hen's finished clucking? Yes? Then let me introduce the Chevaliere to some of our other illustrious guests.
	The crowd parts to reveal CASANOVA, DE SADE, and Ben FRANKLIN.
	d'Eon, may I present the Count Casanova...
CASANOVA	Mi'lady. (*bows*)
LOUIS XVI	...the Marquis de Sade
DE SADE	Enraptured. (*bows*)
LOUIS XVI	...and Mr. Benjamin Franklin of the American colonies.
FRANKLIN	Hello!
ANTOINETTE	(*claps her hands*) What a marvelous opportunity for a little game. Three of

our court's most eligible suitors vying for the hand of one of France's greatest ladies. One, two, three. Which one will you chose to have the first dance with, Mademoiselle? Your choice.

D'EON   (*approaches them*) Hmm. Number one is *very* handsome... and so experienced in the ways of dancing. He would most certainly sweep me off my feet... but... I'm afraid that he would be more concerned with his own reflection in the dance hall mirrors than with my enjoyment.

CASANOVA   It is my loss entirely. (*bows*)

D'EON   Number two is a man of wicked reputation. He dances like a devil unleashed... but... I fear another conflict. Were he to step on my foot, how would I know that he did it accidentally or to satisfy some base sadistic craving?

DE SADE   You'd love every second of it. (*bows*)

D'EON   Which leaves only...

FRANKLIN   C'mon! Let's dance!

> *FRANKLIN pulls her onto the dance floor. They dance.*

D'EON   You are quite a dancer, Mister Franklin.

FRANKLIN   I am accomplished at many things. Why don't you come back to my flat on the East Bank?

D'EON   You are so impetuous. If you're not careful, you Americans are going to gain a reputation.

FRANKLIN   Do I care what a bunch of stuffed powder-puffs think about me? I care this much. (*He snaps his fingers.*) Let's go make love.

D'EON	This is no way to woo a virgin.
FRANKLIN	Fortunately there don't seem to be any virgins present.
D'EON	I am a virgin.
FRANKLIN	You're a virgin? Hah! Everyone knows you French women rut like stoats.

D'EON slaps him.

LOUIS XVI	Here now. What's going on?
FRANKLIN	(*embarrassed*) Begging your pardon, Mademoiselle. (*bows*) I was momentarily distracted by your incredible beauty. Please forgive my impetuousness.
LOUIS XVI	Is everything all right?
D'EON	I forgive you.
LOUIS XVI	Ha ha! A little lover's quarrel perhaps? It would be best not to mess with this hell-cat, Monsieur Franklin. She was quite the swordsman in her day.
D'EON	I still am. Your reputation precedes you, Mister Franklin. I should have been prepared for your abrupt manner. The gossip around court is that you are quite the rake in the salons of Paris.
FRANKLIN	Oh, tongues will wag.
LOUIS XVI	I would like a word with you, d'Eon. You will excuse us, Monsieur?
FRANKLIN	Certainly! I'll see you later, Mademoiselle! (*bows and exits*)
D'EON	What a strange little man.

LOUIS XVI   You will keep your hooks out of him. The fate of our North American interests rest in his lap.

D'EON   You needn't fear any involvement from me.

LOUIS XVI   What's this I see on your dress? You still wear the Croix St. Louis.

D'EON   I earned it, Sire. Why shouldn't I wear it?

LOUIS XVI   This goes against our agreement.

D'EON   Not from my point of view. I wear a dress, as your Majesty has commanded.

LOUIS XVI   It's no secret that you still march about Paris in your Dragoon's costume and you wear this medal in my presence. Are you seeking to provoke me?

D'EON   Certainly not!

LOUIS XVI   Then do as you are told!

> *Light change. Ben FRANKLIN reads from a letter that he has composed to D'EON.*

FRANKLIN   Just a brief note before I head back to America. I hope our little spat didn't put you in a sour pickle. I'm sweet on you, that's all. And I want to extend a personal invitation to you before I leave. Things are heating up across the pond. We're about to kick King George's big fat arse but I need your help to do this. Look, I don't care if you're a woman, you're a damned soldier first. They call you the reincarnation of Joan of Arc! We need that kind of moxy fighting on our side. So, gather up an army of your own. Hell, make 'em all Amazons, I don't care. Just come and fight by my side. Well, I'm gone. Write to me soon. I'm Postmaster General, so it's bound to get to me.

Light change. Another part of the stage.

D'EON   Women of France! When I changed my
wardrobe I did not change my intentions.
I am still a soldier. I am still a patriot. France
has now joined the American War of
Independence against England. Now there
can be no question of my retirement from the
military. This new war represents France's
chance to recover her national honour. I urge
all of you to support my efforts to return to
the dress of a Dragoon captain and apply for
special duty in America!

LOUIS XVI   This time you've gone too far!

D'EON   I have passed successively from the state of a
girl to that of a boy; from the state of a man to
that of a woman. Soon, I hope, with weapons
in my hands, I shall fly on the wings of
Liberty and Victory to fight and die for the
Nation and the Law! My triumph will be
your triumph!

LOUIS XVI   I should have packed you off to a nunnery
years ago.

D'EON   Don't listen to the small men who try to
thwart me.

LOUIS XVI   Small!?

D'EON   For the first time, I am free to admit what was
only whispered rumour. God has revealed it
to me. I am *la pucelle* – the Maid of Orleans!

LOUIS XVI   Alright that's it! I've had enough! Arrest her!
Throw her in chains!

*Soldiers grab D'EON and toss her into a cell.
She prays in prison.*

D'EON   The grace of the Lord will take care of my plight with time, patience, and obedience to the commandments of God. I am content with God, I praise him in all matters, when I look at his radiant face, the bars of my prison melt away.

In a separate area.

ANTOINETTE   You can't treat a woman in this fashion.

LOUIS XVI   She wants to be treated like a man. I only fulfill her wish.

ANTOINETTE   You are a fool!

D'EON is bathed in a holy light.

D'EON   By the grace of God, I am what I am and the grace given to me has not been in vain. God gives everyone a body as He sees fit. It is engulfed in corruption but it will be reborn incorruptible. I am... reborn.

D'EON opens her arms to receive God's blessing.

ANTOINETTE   Look at her! She only gains prestige by sitting in jail. She is the darling of the Paris mob.

LOUIS XVI   Since when did the mob ever concern you?

ANTOINETTE   Open your eyes. Put her under house arrest. Then she'll be out of your way and forgotten as a martyr. Are you listening to me?!

A deep drum beat like the chiming of the clock signifying the start of the Revolution. LOUIS and ANTOINETTE are terrified. They fade into shadow. A man enters D'EON's cell. D'EON prays.

D'EON   The time has finally come.

CLOOTS   Mademoiselle.

D'EON   God grant me the strength to bear the fate
             that my enemies now inflict upon me.

CLOOTS   Excuse me.

D'EON   Perhaps it will be the guillotine. Is that what
             you have in store for me? I know that you
             will protect my soul, even though my body
             will be destroyed. Bless me as I go to the
             stake. In the name of your son, Jesus Christ.
             (*crosses himself*)

                 CLOOTS clears his throat.

             You have come for me.

CLOOTS   Yes... how did you know?

D'EON   It was inevitable. When is it to be?

CLOOTS   When? Immediately.

D'EON   You could have warned me. But that doesn't
             matter. I am ready.

CLOOTS   I have just arrived from Paris.

D'EON   Paris. I see. Where is it to be?

CLOOTS   What?

D'EON   My execution. Will it be in front of the mob?

CLOOTS   ...what execution?

D'EON   You've come to kill me.

CLOOTS   No.

D'EON   Then it will be torture. They are to torture me
             now, Lord!

CLOOTS   I haven't come to torture you, crazy woman.

D'EON   So you are here to torment me with... vile
               words that will...

CLOOTS   No. I am here to set you free.

D'EON   ...I am free?

CLOOTS   France is free. The King is deposed. A
               coalition government has taken his place.

D'EON   But I can't be set free. I am slated for the
               chop.

CLOOTS   Not anymore. You are a free citizen.

D'EON   Then you deny me my martyrdom!

CLOOTS   What?

D'EON   I am to be killed! I must be killed!

CLOOTS   Calm down, woman! Have you eaten some
               bad food? You are free to leave!

D'EON   I must remain in jail. God has ordained it.

CLOOTS   All the other prisoners have been released.
               All the guards have gone home. You would
               be the only tenant.

D'EON   But... I was supposed to... you are a Jacobin?

CLOOTS   You mistake me for one of those crackpots?
               I am Dantonist. I have orders for the release
               of all political prisoners.

D'EON   Then I must proceed to Versailles.

CLOOTS   Versailles is just a sleepy little backwater now.
               The seat of power is in Paris.

D'EON   What am I to do? My King's pension?

CLOOTS	Worthless. If I were you, I would head back to England. With the government in such a flux, it might be wiser to leave this country... at least until our moderate position is strengthened.
D'EON	What shall I do? What has happened to my faith? All signs pointed to my death. I must perish like her. It is ordained. Why has God done this? My Lord! Why have you forsaken me!?
CLOOTS	Control yourself. You must adapt or be swept aside.
D'EON	...I will go to England.
CLOOTS	Come then. Take my hand. It is a beautiful day outside.

Cloots beckons him out as the MACARONI brothers are thrown into the cell by a sadistic jailer.

JAILER	Two Macaronis! Hahahahahaha!

He slams the jail door and exits.

MACARONI 1	Filthy beast!
MACARONI 2	What outrageous treatment!

One of them scrambles to a barred window and tries to peer out. The Paris mob can be heard outside the cell.

Here. Let me stand on your shoulders.

MACARONI 1	Why should it be my shoulders?
MACARONI 2	You are taller and my eyesight is better.
MACARONI 1	God curse your eagle eyes, my brother Macaroni! Very well.

> *MACARONI 2 climbs up precariously with much fussing.*

What do you see? Can you see it from here?

MACARONI 2   Yes. I can see it. They are just in the process of...

> *An abrupt chopping sound – the crowd cheers. MACARONI 2 reels back with a screech and they both tumble to the ground.*

They've chopped someone!

MACARONI 1   Horrors!

> *They sit silent for a second.*

MACARONI 1   So have you heard about d'Eon?

MACARONI 2   Chopped?!

MACARONI 1   No. Got away safely to England, lucky bugger.

> *Another chop. Another cheer.*

They say she is near destitute though. No more King. No more King's pension.

MACARONI 2   At least she still has her neck.

MACARONI 1   Yes. But she has taken to performing in public for money!

MACARONI 2   Disgusting.

MACARONI 1   She gives demonstrations of the sword in full woman's dress!

MACARONI 2   I've never heard the like.

Another chop. Another cheer. The crowd starts to clap in rhythm while shouting "More! More! More!"

JAILER

Macaroniiiiiiiiiiiiis! (*pops his head into the cell*) Hah!

BOTH

Ahhhhhh!

JAILER

Come! Chop-chop-chop, Macaroniiiiiiiiis! Hahahahahah! (*He approaches them menacingly.*)

MACARONI 2

Oh dear. It's all up for the Macaronis. Give me a kiss brother, and then let's defend ourselves.

MACARONI 1 kisses his brother on both cheeks.

JAILER

(*makes kissing sounds*) Kisses! Me too, kiss, kiss, Macaroniiiiiiiiiis! (*He rushes them.*) Ahahahahahahahah!

They flee out the door to the cheers of the crowd. A drum-roll. The MACARONIS can be heard complaining in the distance. A sudden chop! and cheer! Scene changes to England. A crowd files in.

SERVANT

By permission of his Royal Highness the Prince of Wales! For the first time in front of Royalty – Mademoiselle d'Eon's fencing demonstration! Admittance ladies and gentlemen... a mere five shillings!

A cheer as D'EON spots WILKES in the audience.

D'EON

John Wilkes!

WILKES

Shhh. Keep it down. I'm still banished.

D'EON

What are you doing here?

WILKES   I'm here to see you, d'Eon.

              *The PRINCE of Wales stumbles into the
              conversation. He is drunk.*

PRINCE   Who's your friend here, d'Eon?

D'EON   A... Mister Smith, Highness.

PRINCE   Smyth?

WILKES   Yes, Highness.

PRINCE   Going to give d'Eon a go here, Smyth? Eh
              wot? Haw! Haw! Give her a poke! Haw!

WILKES   No, Highness. She's too good for me.

PRINCE   Haw! (*to D'EON*) Why didn't we have you
              fighting on our side in the last war?

D'EON   You didn't ask me, Prince.

PRINCE   Haw! Who's to test the lady then? I'd do
              it myself, but I'm completely foxed. I'd
              probably put out my eye!

              Fawning laughter.

D'EON   Nonsense. I hear that his highness is an
              outstanding swordsman in any condition.

PRINCE   Thank you for saying it. Here's a gold
              sovereign. (*He tosses it at her.*) Who's next
              then? I want to see some more fun.

DRUNK   I'll have a crack at her.

PRINCE   You, sir? You're more plastered than I am.
              Haw, haw!

DRUNK   I don't need to be sober to beat this bitch.

PRINCE   Ho-ho! Are you going to take this insult, d'Eon?

D'EON   Yes, Highness. I will not fight a drunk.

DRUNK   Better a drunk than a freak.

PRINCE   Now, now. Enough rudeness. This is supposed to be a friendly tournament.

DRUNK   She's no friend of mine. This bitch cheated me out of a lot of money.

PRINCE   What?

D'EON   One of the misguided unfortunates who lost a wager on my sex, Highness.

PRINCE   But that was so long ago. The matter is settled now.

DRUNK   It's not fucking settled!

He lunges at D'EON. She steps back and parries easily.

PRINCE   Seize him!

D'EON   No! If we are to do this, then we will do it properly.

She salutes the Prince.

DRUNK   Knock off the fucking pleasantries. Let's fight.

They prepare. A moment of stillness. The DRUNK finds it difficult to maintain his balance. Laughter from the crowd. The opponents cross swords. It is a sloppy fight. D'EON gets the better of him eventually and wounds him lightly to prove a point. General applause. She turns her back to bow and he runs her through. She turns again, seemingly unhurt, and prepares for another round.

During her preparation the sword drops out of D'EON's hands and she collapses. WILKES rushes forward.

D'EON John.

WILKES Don't talk. Preserve your strength.

D'EON It's good to see you again.

WILKES I'll call for a doctor.

D'EON No. I'm fine. See. (*D'EON stands with difficulty.*) Take me home.

WILKES holds D'EON. They walk. Lighting change at D'EON's apartment.

WILKES Not much of a place.

D'EON It's all I can afford.

MRS. COLE Geneviève?

D'EON Yes, it's me. I've brought a friend.

MRS. COLE curtsies.

WILKES She's been hurt.

MRS. COLE Again? Geneviève.

D'EON I know. Just get me some tea.

Mrs. Cole exits.

WILKES Your landlady?

D'EON Roommate. We share the flat.

WILKES smiles.

What?

WILKES	Somehow I never pictured you living as a spinster in a London walk-up.
D'EON	Fortunes change.
WILKES	We'd better have a look.
D'EON	Fucking sleeves. Can't get a decent parry.
WILKES	The dress will have to come off.
D'EON	It'll start to bleed again if I take it off.
WILKES	What kind of life is this, d'Eon?
D'EON	I've been stuck before. I'll lay up in bed for a few days. Then I'll start again.
WILKES	It's madness. You live like a berserker during the day and then at night...
D'EON	What?
WILKES	You turn into my grandmother.
D'EON	No one takes me seriously as a soldier anymore. Performing is the only way I can make money.
WILKES	I have some money for you.
D'EON	It's not Christian to take charity – only to give it.
WILKES	But you're destitute.
D'EON	I did it to myself. Prideful. Just like her.
WILKES	Who?
D'EON	An old acquaintance.

MRS. COLE re-enters with a basin of water and a cloth.

MRS. COLE	Into bed now, Geneviève. I'll bathe that wound.
D'EON	That's won't be necessary. I'll take that. Quit fussing over me.
MRS. COLE	Heavens, you're a stubborn old bag sometimes.
D'EON	I'll be fine. Good night, John.
WILKES	Good night?

D'EON closes the door to his bedroom.

MRS. COLE	Leave her to tend to her wound alone. She's very independent. Would you like some tea?
WILKES	No. I'd better be going.
MRS. COLE	She seemed happy to see you.
WILKES	I'm an old friend.
MRS. COLE	She doesn't have many friends left beside me.
WILKES	You keep each other well?
MRS. COLE	Yes. We're a perfect match. Two grumpy old ladies.
WILKES	I'll say good night then.

WILKES exits. Light change. MRS. COLE observes D'EON. JEANNE d'Arc appears near MRS. COLE.

D'EON	What took you so long?
MRS. COLE	I'm not your servant.
D'EON	You abandoned me.
MRS. COLE	Nonsense.

JEANNE	You didn't need me. So I left.
	MRS. COLE remains in the room tidying up and listening to D'EON's one-sided conversation.
D'EON	We're a fine pair.
MRS. COLE	Yes.
D'EON	I've needed your help.
MRS. COLE	No. You're the most independent soul on earth.
D'EON	You abandoned me and everything fell apart.
JEANNE	That's not what happened. The times changed. That's all. There are no absolutes anymore. I can't exist in such a world. Neither can you.
D'EON	I should have gone out like you.
JEANNE	In a blaze? Yes. That was a real treat for me.
D'EON	I would have endured it.
JEANNE	You! You would have changed your tune the moment the flames started to lick your pretty silk underwear. Count yourself lucky having lived so long.
	D'EON chuckles.
	That's right. You've won. You've outlived them all! You get to hold the pen and tell your story any way you please!
D'EON	(*chuckles*) Are you my guardian angel?
JEANNE	You don't have to stay any longer. Come, take my hand.

Jeanne begins to take D'EON's hand but the friend interrupts.

FRIEND   Any better?

D'EON   Not yet.

                  JEANNE smiles and fades into the background.

MRS. COLE   Near death, poor thing. Come away from her.

                  They move to another section of the stage. A faint moan from D'EON.

FRIEND   Best it's over soon. She's in God's hands.

MRS. COLE   Not without the priest. He promised he'd come today.

FRIEND   He'll be here soon. Anyway, she's tough as an old root. Tea will make it all better. Here.

MRS. COLE   We've been together for so long. Fourteen years.

FRIEND   I'd have troubles living with a Frenchy myself.

MRS. COLE   She's not a Frenchy anymore.

                  Another moan from D'EON.

FRIEND   Sounds like a Frenchy.

MRS. COLE   She's my dearest friend.

D'EON   *(faintly)* Madame.

FRIEND   Calling for you.

MRS. COLE   ...I can't.

FRIEND   I'll go then.

MRS. COLE	Don't disturb her.
FRIEND	What's to disturb? She's out of her wits.
MRS. COLE	Don't touch her.
FRIEND	Come now. You're just as interested as I am.
	The Friend checks for a pulse.
MRS. COLE	Is she gone?
	A Priest pops his head through the door.
PRIEST	Did someone call for a priest?
FRIEND	Too late, Father. (*pulls the sheet over D'EON's head*)
PRIEST	Oh, damn. What a shame. Another soul into perdition thanks to my tardiness.
MRS. COLE	Never. She led a virtuous life. She's flying straight into God's heart this very moment.
PRIEST	Name of the deceased?
MRS. COLE	She was the Chevaliere d'Eon.
PRIEST	Oh, her. By all accounts a very pious woman but...
MRS. COLE	What?
PRIEST	A little tainted with sin because of her deceit. Thirty years of lying. God will figure that onto her ledger.
FRIEND	Let's have a look then!
PRIEST	(*shielding his eyes*) Oh, no, I'd better leave.
FRIEND	Don't leave, Father. You can be a witness. This is history in the making.

MRS. COLE   Let's leave her in peace.

FRIEND   She's going to have to be washed and
wrapped. Everyone will see eventually. Let's
be the first. Come along, Mrs. Cole. You do
the honours.

MRS. COLE   ...very well.

> *The FRIEND raises the sheet and MRS.
> COLE ducks down to look. She looks again to
> make sure then pops her head back up.*

It's so... big!

> *The end.*

Mark Brownell was born in Toronto in 1960. His other plays include *The Blue Wall, Playballs, High Sticking,* and *The Martha Stewart Projects*. He has also written a libretto for a new opera entitled *Iron Road*.

OTHER TITLES
BY MARK BROWNELL

THE BLUE WALL
A collection of monologues about the lives of four
Metro Police officers.
1-55155-660-X $7.00

COACH KINGSTON TELLS IT LIKE IT IS
A crazed coach of a peewee hockey team delivers a pep talk
to the mild-mannered father of one of his players.
In *High Sticking*   1-55155-239-6 $7.00

ELEANOR
A teenage field hockey player confesses while waiting out
a series of penalties on the sidelines.
In *High Sticking*   1-55155-239-6 $7.00

LIFE WITHOUT GRETZKY
A meditation on the selling of Wayne Gretzky to the
Los Angeles Kings.
In *High Sticking*   1-55155-239-6 $7.00

PLAYBALLS
A feisty young woman tries to break into the
male-dominated world of professional umpiring.
1-55173-186-X $7.00

Available from Playwrights Union of Canada
416-703-0201   fax 416-703-0059
orders@puc.ca   http://www.puc.ca

AGMV Marquis

MEMBER OF THE SCABRINI GROUP
Quebec, Canada
2001